About Island Press

Since 1984, the nonprofit organization Island Press has been stimulating, shaping, and communicating ideas that are essential for solving environmental problems worldwide. With more than 1,000 titles in print and some 30 new releases each year, we are the nation's leading publisher on environmental issues. We identify innovative thinkers and emerging trends in the environmental field. We work with world-renowned experts and authors to develop cross-disciplinary solutions to environmental challenges.

Island Press designs and executes educational campaigns in conjunction with our authors to communicate their critical messages in print, in person, and online using the latest technologies, innovative programs, and the media. Our goal is to reach targeted audiences—scientists, policymakers, environmental advocates, urban planners, the media, and concerned citizens—with information that can be used to create the framework for long-term ecological health and human well-being.

Island Press gratefully acknowledges major support of our work by The Agua Fund, The Andrew W. Mellon Foundation, The Bobolink Foundation, The Curtis and Edith Munson Foundation, Forrest C. and Frances H. Lattner Foundation, The JPB Foundation, The Kresge Foundation, The Oram Foundation, Inc., The Overbrook Foundation, The S.D. Bechtel, Jr. Foundation, The Summit Charitable Foundation, Inc., and many other generous supporters.

The opinions expressed in this book are those of the author(s) and do not necessarily reflect the views of our supporters.

Within Walking Distance

Within Walking Distance

CREATING LIVABLE COMMUNITIES FOR ALL

Philip Langdon

Washington | Covelo | London

Island Press is a trademark of The Center for Resource Economics.

Library of Congress Control Number: 2016954340

Printed on recycled, acid-free paper ♺

Manufactured in the United States of America
10 9 8 7 6 5 4 3 2 1

Keywords: Bicycle infrastructure, community development, community investment, gentrification, housing affordability, Lean Urbanism, New Urbanism, pedestrian safety, public transit, public space, safe streets, SmartCode, social capital, Tactical Urbanism, walkability

To Kirk Peterson

Contents

Acknowledgments

Walkable places have long been a passion of mine. In March 1988, I wrote an *Atlantic Monthly* cover story, "A Good Place to Live," about people who were beginning to build new communities in the United States that made walking a central and sociable element of daily life. In the years since, I've written or edited hundreds of articles about human-scale, mixed-use communities, new and old, for a wide range of publications, including ten enjoyable years with editor-publisher Robert Steuteville at his award-winning newsletter, *New Urban News/Better Cities & Towns.*

For quite some time, I've wanted both to distill what I had learned about walkable communities and to dive deeper into a handful of such places, exploring their physical character and their human sides. I am extremely grateful to Richard Oram, who provided crucial financial support for my research and writing through his foundation, the Fund for the Environment and Urban Life.

Heather Boyer, an astute editor at Island Press, brought a much-needed focus and discipline to my sometimes slow and meandering progress. I'm elated that Dhiru A. Thadani, a Washington, DC, architect with a gift for illustration, was willing to produce most of the book's maps and sketches. When Dhiru was called away by other projects, New Haven architect Ben Northrup stepped in with great skill and created the Little Village map and made last-minute refinements to other maps. Elizabeth Farry, editorial assistant at Island Press, proved invaluable in rounding up and organizing photos.

I am grateful to the many people who showed me their communities, familiarized me with local history and local ways of building, explained the workings of neighborhood organizations and municipal governments, and introduced me to residents. Paul Levy and Linda Harris at Philadelphia's Center City District led me to their city's resurgent core neighborhoods and to community groups that have helped those neighborhoods do outstanding things. Thanks especially to Andrew Dalzell and Abby Rambo in Southwest Center City; Janet Finegar and Matt Ruben in Northern Liberties; David Goldfarb, Kandace Gollomp, Dan Pohlig, Dan Rinaldi, Sam Sherman, and Ed and Pam Zenzola in East Passyunk; and Pete Harwan, A. Jordan Rushie, and Isaac F. Slepner in Fishtown. Kevin Gillen, Jennifer Hurley, Alice Ryan, Sandy Sorlien, Murray Spencer, James Wentling, and Inga Saffron, the *Philadelphia Inquirer*'s incisive architecture critic, clued me in to aspects of Philadelphia I otherwise might have missed.

In New Haven, Mark Abraham, Will Baker, Ka Wa Chan, Pino Ciccone, Louise deCarrone, Anstress Farwell, Matthew Feiner, Barbara Folsom, Robert Frew, Eva Geertz, Chris George, Seth Godfrey, Bill Kaplan, Joel LaChance, Joe Puleo, Deborah Rossi, Giuseppe and Rosanna Sabino, Lisa Siedlarz, Romeo Simeone, Kevin Sullivan, Melanie Taylor, and Claudia Wielgorecki all expanded my knowledge of East Rock. Also helpful on New Haven were Frank Pannenborg, Patrick Pinnell, and Clay Williams.

Donna Simons and Robert Stevens in Brattleboro, Vermont, and Daniel Scully in Keene, New Hampshire, helped me make contacts in

Brattleboro and get an overall sense of the town. In Brattleboro and vicinity, I learned much from Pal Barofsky, Matthew Blau, Pierre Capy, Wes Cutting, Peter Elwell, Alex Gyori, Parker Huber, Dylan Mackinnon, Joelle Montagnino, Orly Munzing, Paul Putnam, Connie Snow, Jeanne Walsh, Allyson Wendt, Bob Woodworth, Greg Worden, and Benjamin Zeman.

In Chicago, Ruth Knack, editor for many years of my articles in *Planning Magazine*, made me feel at home. Andrea Muñoz was a magnificent guide to Little Village, introducing me to Simone Alexander, the Reverend Tom Boharic, Matt DeMateo, Jaime di Paulo, Jesus Garcia, Maria Herrera, Cristel Kolmeder, Ricardo Muñoz, Mike Rodriguez, Ciria Ruiz, Kim Wasserman, and others. Scott Bernstein, Matt Cole, Larry Lund, Dominic Pacyga, Carmen Prieto, and Emily Talen also shared their Chicago insights.

In Portland, Oregon, Bruce Allen, David and Anita August, Patricia Gardner, Randy Gragg, Rick Gustafson, Ed McNamara, Michael Mehaffy, Ethan Seltzer, Al Solheim, Bruce Stephenson, and Kate Washington instructed me in many facets of the Pearl District. Thanks also go to Allan Classen, Carolyn Ciolkosz, Joe Cortright, Dick Harmon, Steve Reed Johnson, Rodney O'Hiser, Steve Rudman, Tiffany Sweitzer, Elise Wagner, and Homer Williams.

In Starkville, Mississippi, Dan Camp and Neil Strickland gave me hours of their time. Mary Lee Beal, Briar Jones, Lynn Spruill, Parker Wiseman, and an observant visiting professor from Notre Dame, Philip Bess, were among the many others who aided my study of the Cotton District.

Peter Chapman, Steve Culpepper, Jennifer Griffin, Richard J. Jackson, Scot Mackinnon, Alan Mallach, Arthur C. Nelson, and Jeff Speck all helped along the way. I thank Kirk Peterson, my friend for fifty years, for riding the overnight train from upstate New York to Chicago to do Spanish-English translation for me in Little Village.

Thanks also go to the many individuals and organizations that allowed me to reproduce their photographs, including Bruce Forster Photography; Friends of Chester Arthur; Steven Koch, Koch Landscape Architecture; Gerding Edlen; Little Village Environmental Justice Organization; Peter Mauss, Esto Photographics, courtesy of Gossens Bachman Architects; Jeremy Murdock, courtesy of The Cotton District; Hannah O'Connell, Town of Brattleboro; PhillyHistory.org; Leslie Schwartz; Robert Stevens; and Benjamin Zeman, Mocha Joe's Roasting Company.

Most of all, I am grateful to my wife, Maryann Langdon, for seeing me through the many ups and downs of this challenging project.

Introduction

Janet Finegar was talking about the park in her neighborhood, and it was beginning to sound as if the park were a member of her family, maybe a precocious son or perhaps a daughter who was a musical prodigy. "My beloved child," Finegar said more than once when describing Liberty Lands, a two-acre park that she, as much as anyone, had created from a wasteland of industrial rubble.

Finegar lives in Northern Liberties, a section of Philadelphia that as recently as the 1990s was bounteously supplied with rubble. Tanneries, cigar factories, breweries, a factory that made records (vinyl ones), and other industries had mostly cleared out of Northern Liberties, leaving the two-third-square-mile corner of Philly for the next generation—Finegar's generation—to come and set it right.

She and her neighbors did exactly that. In an urban precinct that had no parks, they built one on their own. Now it was flourishing. After two decades of volunteer labor contributed by people who could walk to the park from their homes, Liberty Lands had a butterfly garden, a Native American garden, a community garden, 180 trees of varied species, picnic benches, a mural depicting birds and bees, and open

1

grassland. It had become the centerpiece of a neighborhood that is gaining population faster than any other in Philadelphia. Today, Finegar, who lives with her husband and teenaged daughter in a rowhouse not far away, continues volunteering about fifteen hours a week to keep the park appealing.

"It's a great thing," she said about the park. "It solidifies everything that goes on in the neighborhood." In a video that you can find online, she summed up a lesson that Liberty Lands had taught her: "We all need to settle in a little bit and love our places and know our places and work to make them better."[1]

Finegar is one of the many remarkable individuals I encountered during my search to understand what it is like to live in America's walkable communities. Specifically, I wondered how pedestrian-scale places benefit their residents, how residents confront problems, and what people do to help these places improve.

In Little Village, a Mexican American section of the Southwest Side of Chicago, I talked with Rob Castañeda as he took a break by the playground outside Ortiz de Dominguez Elementary School. "This location is on the border between the Latin Kings and the Two Six gang," he told me. "This is where people got shot, stabbed. Got jumped. Then in 2006, we started a program for families. Families would come and play games, schoolyard games. There might be kite-building. A thousand people came for a picnic for kindergarten, first-, and second-grade participants."

Castañeda founded and runs Beyond the Ball, a sports-based program designed to teach personal and social responsibility. He uses it to steer boys in Little Village—an immigrant neighborhood that has numerous positive things, including corner stores, street vendors, block clubs, and one of the biggest-selling retail corridors in Chicago—away from gangs, which recruit kids when they are around fifth or sixth grade. "The gang issue," said Castañeda, "is the number one issue in this community."

Rob Castañeda outside Ortiz de Dominguez Elementary School on South
Lawndale Avenue near West Thirty-First Street in Chicago's Little Village.
The community reclaimed the street corner from violence, converting it into a
popular recreation area. Castañeda founded an organization called Beyond the
Ball to help boys around fifth and sixth grades resist gang life. (Photo by Philip
Langdon)

The corner of South Lawndale Avenue and West Thirty-First Street adjacent to the school has been transformed from a place of aggression and intimidation into a popular recreation space. "We put in a soccer field," Castañeda said. "Our kids needed a space where they could thrive." He is one of the many people who are using public spaces—including streets, sidewalks, parks, gardens, and school grounds—to enhance the lives of Little Village's nearly 80,000 inhabitants.

Walkable communities come in many sizes and complexions. They span the economic spectrum and face a wide assortment of challenges, but one strength many of them share is a capacity for bringing people together: both to combat social ills and to make daily life more rewarding. In the East Rock section of New Haven, Connecticut, I met with Eva Geertz, a writer and former bookseller, to find out why she is fiercely attached to her neighborhood and how she incorporates its numerous small, independent grocery stores and cafes into her ambles around town.

East Rock's food stores are a world apart from the big supermarkets. "At the Orange Street Market, they have a real butcher, Jimmy the butcher," Geertz said. "If you have a side of beef, Jimmy Apuzzo would carve it for you. Jimmy is good. Jimmy is awesome. I do believe that when you buy ground beef there, it's not coming from seventeen different cows. He's grinding it himself."

Little neighborhood grocery stores can be expensive, but Geertz has mastered the art of shopping thriftily and coming home with things of quality. Walking through East Rock and downtown, "I always have a giant bag, ready to pick things up," she said. She checks out nearly all the stores. When she stops at Romeo & Cesare's, a grocery store operated by burly Romeo Simeone, who speaks with Italian-inflected English and has opera playing in the background, she basks in the store's personality. "Romeo's is really family-oriented. Romeo wants to say hello to all the babies. Fran, his daughter, knows their names," she said.

If some things do cost more than Geertz would like, there is the compensation of knowing that she is saving money by not driving. "I actively hate being behind the wheel," she emphasized. "The walkable city: it's not a trivial thing."

What these three individuals in Philadelphia, Chicago, and New Haven expressed to me was the satisfaction they get from being part of a walkable community, where there are many ways to get to know people and where one person can often make a genuine difference. A lot of professional publications tell how to plan streets and sidewalks that pedestrians like to use, how to design buildings that make the public spaces convivial, and how to change government rules so that the things people want within walking distance are allowed to be there. I draw from those sources, of course, but what I most wanted to explore is the human element.

I decided to acquaint myself with several places that contain at least the basic elements of a walkable community, explain how they have been shaped, and review what the results have been for their residents. Not surprisingly, I learned that local governments have a crucial role to play, but I also came away with a greater appreciation of neighborhood associations, groups of local merchants, business improvement districts, volunteer organizations, and—most of all—civic-minded individuals, including artists, architects, entrepreneurs, homeowners, and renters. The thinking and imagination that this tremendously varied bunch of people have devoted to making walkable communities work for us all are captured in the pages that follow.

The Direction of History

For five thousand years, human settlements were nearly always compact places. The things a person needed on a regular basis lay within walking distance. At the end of the eighteenth century, it took about an hour to go on foot from the southern edge of Philadelphia, the second-largest city in the United States, to its northern edge. The distance was 2.7 miles.[2]

Building a city or town at the scale of the pedestrian meant that any able-bodied person could navigate the full range of local businesses, homes, institutions, and attractions without relying on anything more than his or her own power. Philadelphia, according to urban historian Sam Bass Warner Jr., "functioned as a single community."[3] It was not necessary to own a horse or an ox cart—or, later, a motor vehicle—to participate in the life of the town. The built environment and the human body were in accord.

Conditions have changed radically over two hundred years. Large increases in population and capital and a torrent of innovation led many influential individuals—Henry Ford and Frank Lloyd Wright among them—to see the walkable community as obsolete and not particularly desirable. Modern humans were destined to be masters of distance. Ford, Wright, and Le Corbusier, the French-Swiss architect who did more than anyone else to establish the Modern movement in architecture, all favored an automobile-dependent way of life.

"Everywhere the great problem of modern times is the reconstitution of the street pattern for automobiles in a vastly larger network," Le Corbusier declared. The automobile "cannot live" in a traditional urban plan; it needed to be able to move fast, "without stops."[4] Le Corbusier advocated the machine city, made up of components physically segregated from one another.[5] In the late nineteenth century, this idea—that the basics of daily life no longer needed to be clustered tightly together—began to catch on, first in Germany and then in Britain and the United States.

Propaganda, some of it commissioned by the petroleum industry, encouraged the public to yearn for something other than pedestrian-scale communities. In 1937, for a public relations project sponsored by Shell Oil Company, Norman Bel Geddes, an industrial designer with a flair for getting a message across, built a scale model of "the automotive city of tomorrow." Strikingly designed, the model aimed to persuade the public—which had been outraged at the number of pedestrians killed each year by motor vehicles—to embrace a vision of fast highways miraculously threaded through dense communities. Shell bought advertising in the *Saturday Evening Post,* the best-loved magazine of its day, to present photos of the mesmerizing model and to portray Bel Geddes as an "authority on future trends." "Bel Geddes's model became motordom's manifesto," said technology historian Peter Norton, author of the revelatory book *Fighting Traffic.*[6] Bel Geddes dubbed his mobility concept "magic motorways" and went on to design General Motors Corporation's Futurama exhibit at the New York World's Fair of 1939, one of the most effective public relations extravaganzas of the twentieth century.

By separating land uses into separate zones, governments made automobile use almost a requirement of modern living. "Separation of uses" had been seen as a way of keeping noisy, soot-producing industry apart from residential neighborhoods, but it eventually kept multifamily housing away from single-family houses and kept stores and taverns apart from residential subdivisions. With cars to transport them, middle- and upper-income families could settle at lower density, in houses with lawn on all sides.

Some places became quieter and more tranquil but also duller and more inconvenient; many goods, services, and activities could no longer be found close at hand. Variety, long a hallmark of urban life, shrank. Neighborhoods "protected" by zoning became more costly to live in, not only because of restrictions on what could be built, but also because each household felt compelled to buy a car, or maybe two or three, to make the distended geography function.

In these pages, I show that places where the best of life is within walking distance ought to be our goal. I started to write in favor of pedestrian-scale development in the 1980s and found like-minded souls in the nascent New Urbanism movement, composed of designers, builders, developers, and citizens who wanted to create or live in compact communities where a person could get somewhere useful on foot.[7] After fierce initial resistance from much of the homebuilding industry, the tide started to turn. Battery Park City in New York showed that new large-scale development could be organized on a traditional street grid, interspersed with small parks. Near downtown Denver, Highlands' Garden Village, a compact neighborhood with cafes, shops, a farmers' market, and offices, was built on the grounds of an abandoned amusement park.[8] Several hundred human-scale, mixed-use suburban developments, from Kentlands in Gaithersburg, Maryland, to Orenco Station in Hillsboro, Oregon, west of Portland, came into being.

Projects like those required substantial capital, however, and when the housing downturn of 2007 and the economic crisis of 2008 brought development practically to a standstill, it became clear that the walkable communities Americans were most interested in were not suburban traditional neighborhood developments; they were old city neighborhoods, downtowns, former industrial precincts, and compact first-ring suburbs. Young people flocked to urban neighborhoods where coffeehouses, bars, stores, music venues, and other amenities could be reached on foot. So did a considerable number of baby boomers and retirees. Residents who had lived in those neighborhoods for years had already done much to fix up some of them. What were these urban-dwellers finding?

In these pages are the stories of six places that differ in size, history, wealth, and education yet share certain traits. Most importantly, they are all densely settled; they have a mix of uses and activities; they have extensively connected streets; and they relate well to the human eye, human size, and human gait.

Philadelphia is a city predominantly of pedestrian-scale rowhouses and town-houses that give a sense of enclosure to narrow streets. The silhouette in the background is City Hall, topped by a statue of William Penn. (Drawing by Dhiru A. Thadani)

I open with Center City Philadelphia because I have been visiting Philadelphia since the late 1960s, in bad times and in good, and have been impressed by the blossoming of neighborhoods both in and just beyond the city's core. Next I focus on the East Rock section of New Haven, Connecticut, the neighborhood I have lived in for a third of a century. In particular, I look at how East Rock has created a series of outdoor and indoor gathering places, dramatically changing the atmosphere of the neighborhood's central corridor and fostering a new gregariousness.

I then turn to Brattleboro, Vermont, an old community of 12,000 people whose Main Street business district has been tenaciously defended by residents, merchants, artists, and government. In Brattleboro, people band together to do remarkable things when challenged, whether by a fire that wrecked a landmark building or by a big-box chain that threatened the livelihood of the downtown hardware store.

If communities with walkable traits work, they should serve not only middle- and upper-income people but also minorities and people of modest means. With that in mind, I examine how Chicago's Little Village, the largest Mexican American community in the Midwest, draws strength from the Chicago street grid, a dense population, experienced community organizers, and the talents of mural painters, among others. Little Village has created new parks, built new schools, counteracted gangs, and, during a relentless heat wave, kept vulnerable elderly residents alive.

Next is the Pearl District in Portland, Oregon, where a network of small blocks, many of them carved out of a former rail yard, contains buildings old and new, including housing, retail, offices, and cultural institutions. In my judgment, the Pearl District is the most outstanding edge-of-downtown district created in any US city since the beginning of the New Urbanism movement. A long-term agreement between the city and a major developer led to development of a streetcar line, new parks, and a substantial volume of affordable housing.

Finally, I tell the story of the Cotton District in Starkville, Mississippi, where one man, Dan Camp, who started out as an instructor of shop teachers, transformed a dilapidated ten-block area over more than forty years. The Cotton District, formerly a leftover part of town, has now become the liveliest neighborhood in Starkville.

Each of these six communities sheds light on how a neighborhood, district, or town recognizes problems, identifies opportunities, and marshals its resources. Together, they show why people choose to live in walkable communities, what they do for their communities, and how those places can get better as time goes by.

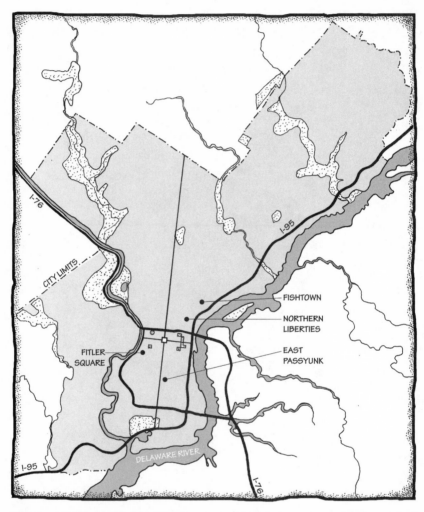

The city of Philadelphia, showing its principal highways, major parks, the original five squares, and a few of its walkable central neighborhoods. (Drawing by Dhiru A. Thadani)

CHAPTER 1

Big City, Intimate Settings: Center City Philadelphia

I became fascinated by Philadelphia long ago for the simplest of reasons: in my youth, I was a Pennsylvanian to the core. I was enthusiastic about the state's beautiful topography, proud of its industrial accomplishments, and eager to learn its history. I grew up in the opposite corner of Pennsylvania from Philadelphia, first in Greenville, a manufacturing and college town where my father was city editor of the local newspaper, and then, after he died at age forty-seven, in the Erie area when my mother remarried and we moved in with her new husband. I remained in northwestern Pennsylvania through graduation from Allegheny College in June 1969. Five days later, I started my first full-time job, as a reporter for the *Patriot-News* in Harrisburg, 250 miles to the southeast.

Philadelphia, then the fourth-most-populous city in the nation (it is now fifth), lay only 100 miles farther east. So, on one of my first weekends off, I headed for the city that had been home to Benjamin Franklin, Robert Morris, and other history-making figures. In the years since, I have returned countless times.

My first impression of Philadelphia was that everything was crammed together. The city's 142 square miles were densely filled with buildings of all kinds, but especially with rowhouses: attached dwellings two, three, and sometimes four stories high. Philadelphians erected their first row-houses near the banks of the Delaware less than a decade after William Penn's 1682 founding of the commonwealth, and they never stopped building them.[1] There was block after block after block of rowhouses, confining in their narrowness, I thought at the time, yet economical, efficient, and comforting in their own way. In a rowhouse neighbor-hood, many of the things a person needs are within walking distance.

In Center City Philadelphia—the business and historic hub between the Delaware and Schuylkill Rivers—the typical rowhouse is 12 to 16 feet wide. The most luxurious, called townhouses, are 18 to 22 feet wide. Standing shoulder to shoulder, the rows of attached houses come within 6 to 10 feet of the street, as if part of their job is to keep watch over the public realm. The streets themselves are compact, some so nar-row that they accommodate only one lane of moving vehicles.

For a long time, I wondered how a city so densely populated—at its peak in 1950, Philadelphia had more than 2 million inhabitants—could function with streets so minuscule. The street network seemed antique, and traffic often moved slowly. I had spent the first 22 years of my life in the northwestern part of the state, however, where things were more spread out and people took it for granted that you would have an automo-bile. Perhaps I needed to start viewing things from a different perspective.

Eventually, I realized that judging a big city like Philadelphia—indeed, any city—by the speed at which motor vehicles cruise the streets made little sense. In Philadelphia, people got around on foot and in Southeastern Pennsylvania Transit Authority (SEPTA) buses, subways, streetcars, and commuter trains, not solely in automobiles. Today they continue to use all those modes of transportation, except now many of them also bike. In a well-functioning city, the automobile is just one means of transportation, and it is not the best.

I learned that narrow streets and continuous rows of buildings can give a neighborhood intimacy. In most of the central neighborhoods, stores, cafes, and parks are within walking distance. People circulate on foot, which helps them make friends with people nearby. Compactness helps breed tight-knit neighborhoods.

When population density is high enough, a neighborhood can support commercial enterprises within walking distance, such as coffee places, cafes, taverns, dry cleaners, and convenience stores. Some are likely to be franchises, but Center City has many locally owned businesses that reflect the proprietor's personality. One evening, a friend and I dined at a little restaurant in Washington Square West. It was a BYOB establishment with no liquor license, so I stopped beforehand at a corner store that packed a large variety of beers into a very small space and took some to the restaurant. The idiosyncrasies of the neighborhood made it fun. It was a far cry from the experience of driving along a suburban roadside and choosing from the same chain restaurants you have seen in a hundred other locales.

In cities and towns that were laid out for automobiles, distances dull the experience and make it unlikely you will see someone on the street and launch a conversation then and there. Center City, by contrast, fits everyday activities into walking trips along streets where you can meet people. Because of its human scale, Center City attracts a growing number of people who are tired of cars and the car-dependent lifestyle. Ivelisse Cruz, in her midtwenties, moved to Southwest Center City because, she said, "I got a job at the University of Pennsylvania and I wanted to walk to work. I didn't want to deal with the frustrations of traffic. Walking, it's about 25 to 35 minutes to my office on the western edge of UPenn. I have a car, but I use it once a week, if that."

Jason Duckworth, president of Arcadia Land Company, a real estate developer, moved from Narbeth, a century-old railroad suburb in Montgomery County, northwest of Philadelphia, to the Logan Square section of Center City because he and his wife wanted to be in an urban setting, wanted to walk, and thought the move would benefit their school-age daughters, who are both now enrolled at Masterman, a public magnet school they reach on foot. "These city middle-schoolers know how to ride SEPTA, where to find the best chocolate chip cookie, where to hang out with a friend over a slice of pizza," Duckworth said. "They get to have more independence than was possible in Narbeth, though Narbeth is pretty darn good as far as suburbs go.

"It was especially important for us," he said, "that they live with people different from them—different races, different economic situations, different religions—and, through that, perhaps be more empathetic and more open to experience. It reminds me of the famous Louis Kahn line about kids and cities: 'A city is the place of availabilities. It is the place where a small boy, as he walks through it, may see something that will tell him what he wants to do with his whole life.'"

Some gravitate to walkable neighborhoods even when their jobs are miles away. Ajinkya Joglekar, who works in Wilmington, Delaware, and his wife, Joanna, who works in a northwest Philadelphia suburb, bought a newly built three-story rowhouse in Southwest Center City because they could travel by train and end each day in a friendly, compact place where neighbors know one another. "It's great being able to step out the front door and walk two blocks for a beer and burger," said Ajinkya Joglekar, who is in his early thirties. "At the Grays Ferry Triangle [on South Street], 5 minutes away, we've met a lot of people." Joanna Joglekar regards walking to the Thirtieth Street Station as "my built-in exercise" and likes shopping in walkable places. "We shop more small business than big box. I feel the quality of products is better," she said.

The city's core has a few wide thoroughfares. Broad Street, which runs north and south from City Hall, and Market Street, which crosses Broad at City Hall, are 100 feet wide from building face to building face; those two streets would feel daunting if they did not have buildings several stories high—buildings tall enough to give the street a sense of enclosure—facing them. Still, most streets—even lively commercial ones—are fairly narrow, making them easy to cross. Street corners are very tight; they are not the sweeping curves that have become commonplace—and dangerous—in modern suburbs. Intersections with hardly any curve force vehicles to slow down before they turn, which is better for pedestrians. Traditional urban features—narrow streets; tight, right-angled intersections; short blocks; frequent doorways; lots of human-size windows; and a mix of uses within walking distance—persuade people to travel on foot or by bicycle, bus, or trolley to stores, restaurants, offices, cultural events, and all sorts of destinations.

What happened? Why did Center City deteriorate? And how did it get its groove back?

How Center City Declined and Revived

In the opening decades of the twentieth century, Philadelphia was a city of diverse and thriving industries. Civic boosters called it the Workshop of the World. At the time of its industrial peak in 1953, roughly 395,000 Philadelphians—45 percent of the labor force—made their living in manufacturing. In the decades that followed, however, industry contracted radically. By 2011, fewer than 30,000 industrial jobs remained, amounting to a mere 5 percent of the city's employment.[2] Areas that depended on factory jobs, especially in North Philadelphia, decayed.

In the 1960s and 1970s, crime exploded and racial tension deepened, conditions that, when combined with the disappearance of industrial jobs, prompted hundreds of thousands of white people to move out of the city. The early 1990s was another tough period, with a crack cocaine epidemic near its height. Drug abuse plus turf wars among the suppliers triggered a wave of violent crime. Buzz Bissinger's book *A Prayer for the City* ably chronicles the desperation of Philadelphia in that period.[3]

Against that backdrop, the recovery of Center City since then is

Rodman Street near South Twelfth Street in Center City around the early 1960s, when many of the nineteenth-century rowhouses stood abandoned. This block is now a tidy, safe area where families with children choose to live. (Photo courtesy of PhillyHistory.org, a project of the Philadelphia Department of Records)

nothing less than astonishing. Philadelphia's central business district went from severe distress in 1990 to good condition in 2010, by which time it had amassed the third-largest residential population of any business center in the United States. Center City Philly ranks behind only two business districts—Midtown Manhattan and Downtown Manhattan—in number of residents.[4] The city's core gained population even while areas like North Philadelphia remained depressed.

There are three main reasons for Center City's resurgence, First, Center City and some of its peripheral areas abound with jobs in two booming sectors of the US economy: medicine and higher education. Education and health care institutions have become the backbone of Philadelphia's economy, providing 36 percent of the city's jobs. Nearly 60 percent of the region's education and health care employment is in the city, with much of it clustered in Center City, University City (the area west of the Schuylkill that is home to the University of Pennsylvania, Drexel University, and hospitals), and North Philadelphia (the base of Temple University).[5]

Second, Center City's compactness and intermixing of uses were never fatally undone by urban renewal. "Philadelphia has a certain genius for not doing things," said urban historian and former Philadelphian Robert Fishman. "A lot of wonderful stuff would have been knocked down in

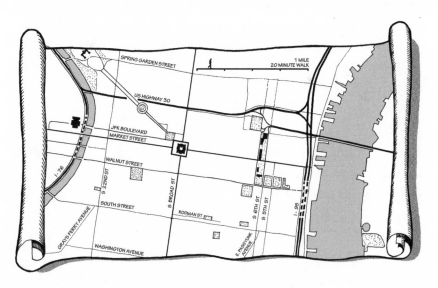

Greater Center City, showing some of its major streets, plus Rodman Street, a narrow side street that has gone from semiabandonment in the 1960s to desirability today. From the Delaware River to the Schuylkill is about a 40-minute walk. (Drawing by Dhiru A. Thadani)

the 1950s and 1960s as part of urban renewal or just the general corpo-
ratization of downtown. Some of that happened, such as Penn Center,
the worst of the Rockefeller Center wannabes, or Market East. But a
whole lot, like the South Street Expressway, never happened. Enough
survived to be the basis for revival in the 1970s and afterwards."

Third, crime and disorder have been dealt with energetically and
often intelligently. In Center City, serious crimes declined 52 percent
from 1991 to 2015.[6]

The heart of Philadelphia has fared so well that the boundaries of
Center City have pushed outward. In the 1960s, Center City—the
downtown plus a number of neighborhoods nearby—ended around
Vine Street on the north and around South Street on the south. In general, the areas beyond Vine or South lay outside the orbit of Center City.
By the mid-1970s, however, many people in peripheral neighborhoods
like Northern Liberties and parts of South Philadelphia wanted to be
associated with the city's center. Real estate pages in the city's newspa-
pers started identifying houses north of Vine or south of South as Center City properties, and over the next four decades, those neighborhoods
became increasingly integrated into the city's core.[7]

Clean and Safe

James Wentling, an architect with an office near City Hall, recalled
Center City in the 1980s: "There was a very high amount of panhandling, begging, people lying in the streets." Then the situation began
to change. A publicity-shy real estate developer, Ronald Rubin, whose
family company controlled more property than anyone else downtown,
started a drive in 1990 to establish a business improvement district,
paid for by property owners. It would be called the Center City District
and would focus at first on two goals: making the downtown *clean* and
making it *safe*. The Center City District (CCD) began operation in
the spring of 1991 with a $6.5 million budget and with programs and

services defined by a board of directors entirely from the private sector. The CCD hired workers to clean the sidewalks and employed "safety ambassadors," employees who helped the public, watched for threatening activities, and called the police when necessary. As time went on, the CCD set about marketing Center City and improving the streetscape. For businesspeople like Rubin, the CCD was a means of making a languishing, unkempt Center City appealing and competitive, thus generating tenants and profits for real estate interests while also benefiting institutions, city government, and the residents themselves, many of whom were troubled by how far conditions had degenerated.[8]

This clean and safe campaign went a long way toward steadying the downtown's atmosphere. In two decades, serious crime was cut by half, and quality-of-life offenses were reduced by three-quarters. Paul Levy, executive director of the CCD since its inception, sees the district as "a textbook case of how to nudge a place over the tipping point."[9]

Along with a stable and safer downtown, Philadelphia needed better leadership in government than in the past. It got it from Edward Rendell, a gravelly voiced former district attorney who in 1991 was elected to the first of two four-year terms as mayor. Rendell told me, "I wanted to bring back the city in general. We had to start with downtown. We had to reclaim our streets downtown." To that end, he increased patrols in Center City's two police districts, with guidance from the CCD's safety ambassadors. One Rendell tactic involved having the police maintain a safe walking corridor between the convention center and the downtown hotels. As time went by, an expanding area benefited from this policy.

In the 1990s, homelessness and panhandling had become chronic in urban centers across the nation. Rendell responded with a measured policy: moving homeless individuals off the streets and nudging them toward a way of living that would be better for themselves and for the city. Many of the homeless "are mentally ill and afraid to go into homeless shelters," Rendell said. "I told the police: Move them, put them in

Measuring the Walkable Community

The Charter of the New Urbanism states that "many activities of daily living should occur within walking distance, allowing independence to those who do not drive, especially the elderly and the young."[a] New Urbanists try to make sure that the most important everyday destinations are within a fourth of a mile, or a 5-minute walk. Some destinations, like those needed by small children, should be even closer. The SmartCode (a form-based code originally conceived by the Miami architecture and planning firm Duany Plater-Zyberk & Company), for example, calls for some kind of play space within 800 feet of every dwelling. For convenience to transportation, transit planners often aim for a walking distance of 10 or even 15 minutes to higher-speed transit, like rail, but a closer, 5-minute walking distance to bus stops.

In 2007, Jesse Kocher and Matt Lerner in Seattle developed a tool for calculating how walkable any area is. They named it Walk Score and distributed it through a company bearing that name. In Walk Score, locations are rated from zero to one hundred. The highest ratings are awarded to addresses or neighborhoods where amenities of various kinds are within one-fourth of a mile. In recent years, Walk Score has also introduced a transit score and a bike score, which evaluate how easy or difficult it is for people to carry out everyday errands on a bicycle or public transit.

I went to the company's website (walkscore.com) and typed in "Fitler Square Philadelphia," the name of a Center City neighborhood. I learned that Fitler Square had a near-perfect Walk Score of 96. It is a place where "daily errands do not require a car" according to the website. "There are about 200 restaurants, bars and coffee shops in Fitler Square," Walk Score reported. "People in Fitler Square can walk to an average of 24 restaurants, bars and coffee shops in 5 minutes." Fitler Square also got a transit score of 99 and a bike score of 99.

Walk Score helps people get a sense of how walkable various neighborhoods are. Planners, urban designers, public health specialists, and civic activists have begun employing its maps and calculations to improve physical conditions and to incorporate walking into people's daily routines. The City of Phoenix used Walk Score data to see where long blocks and superblocks should be broken up, especially near future stations of the Metro Light Rail System.[b]

---

[a] Principle 10 in "The Neighborhood, the District, and the Corridor," *Charter of the New Urbanism*, https://www.cnu.org/who-we-are/charter-new-urbanism.

[b] Philip Langdon, "Walk Score Could Lead to Better-Planned Transit Networks," *New Urban News*, Sept. 2011, p. 7, http://bettercities.net/article/walk-score-could-lead-better-planned-transit-networks-15280.

If you drill down far enough, you will find aspects of Walk Score that are ambiguous or misleading. Walk Score's metrics do not take into account some of the urban design features that make a pedestrian-friendly setting. Jorge L. Simbaqueba, a transportation engineer and graduate researcher at the University of Connecticut, said that among the features left out are sidewalks of comfortable width, in good repair, shaded in hot weather; planter strips where they are appropriate; and building setbacks that enhance the public realm.

Despite its limitations, Walk Score has improved public understanding of walkability. "The cities with the highest Walk Score ratings—New York, San Francisco, Boston, Philadelphia—are indeed the most walkable," said New Urbanist writer and editor Robert Steuteville.[c] So, use Walk Score, but also spend time looking at the neighborhood itself. Observe whether its walking routes are comfortable. Confirm that the amenities there are ones you find useful. Ask local people how dependable the transit system is, or ride it yourself. Walk Score is a good snapshot, but it is not the definitive answer.

Trees and other vegetation soften a street of rowhouses in Center City's Fitler Square neighborhood. On some blocks, portions of the sidewalk are brick, accentuating the setting's human scale. (Photo by Philip Langdon)

[c] Robert Steuteville, "The Problem with Walk Score," *Better Cities & Towns*, Sept. 1, 2015, http://bettercities.net/news-opinion/blogs/robert-steuteville/21738/problem -walk-score.

your car, but don't arrest them." Officers transported homeless individuals to shelters. Some of them agreed to enter the shelters. "Eventually," said Rendell, "they stopped panhandling." Also, the public had to be persuaded to stop behaving in ways that fostered begging and other negative activity. "These well-meaning groups from the suburbs would feed [homeless individuals] on the streets," Rendell noted. "I said I don't want you feeding them on the street any more. We have good soup kitchens, etc.... I got them to back off. The problem in the feeding is that they litter and they also go to the bathroom on the outside. We used food as a hook to get them into drug treatment and job training."

Levy credits Rendell, whose successes in Philadelphia propelled him to eight years as governor, with rethinking how government agencies spend money to help the needy. Philadelphia, Levy said, upped its spending on services connected with homelessness from $42 million a year to $108 million a year. The city shifted toward a more extended network of help, including drug and alcohol treatment, and brought a higher level of coordination to the services. "Special teams were funded for the police," Levy noted. They would tell people, "You can't lie here, you can't sleep here. Here's a way of getting help." As a result, he said, "We went from 400 sleeping on the streets to 100 sleeping on the streets." The "continuum of care" approach has worked well, he said, for just about everyone except those with severe mental illinesses, such as paranoid schizophrenia. In 2008, an organization known as Pathways to Housing PA instituted a "Housing First" approach, which offers apartments to those with psychiatric disabilities, and supplements it with treatment services covering mental and physical health, substance abuse, education, and employment. The strategy seems to have worked.[10] Some of Philadelphia's recent mayors have not been as attentive to problems like panhandling and sleeping in public places as Rendell was, but the conditions they faced were much better than in the early 1990s.

A city cannot be walkable and livable if many of its buildings are

neglected and unoccupied. In 1997, Philadelphia started offering property tax abatements to owners who would convert vacant buildings
to residential use, anywhere in the city. In 2000, the incentives were
expanded to new construction. These policies helped bring on a housing boom. "In 1990, there was just one major residential condominium
in the commercial core," Levy pointed out. "Now, there are 49 condominium buildings with 3,871 units and another 165 apartment buildings with 15,630 units, in what had been purely a commercial district."

Over the years, the CCD has made $118 million in streetscape and
public area enhancements, paid for by CCD bond issues and through
leverage of city, state, federal, and foundation funds. The quality of
the environment has been upgraded by 1,000 new street trees, 2,200
pedestrian-scale light fixtures, nearly 700 maps and directional signs
for pedestrians, and 233 maps and signs for motorists. On a section of
Broad Street that was rechristened Avenue of the Arts, synchronized,
color-changing lights enliven the facades of buildings.[11]

The city carried out demolition and reconstruction where no practical alternative existed. In 1999, four towers containing 576 public
housing units in Martin Luther King Plaza, situated in the Hawthorne
neighborhood southeast of Center City, were dynamited. The towers
had for years been a cradle of drug addiction, crime, and poverty, causing distress for the neighborhood. Through the federal HOPE VI public
housing redevelopment program, the Philadelphia Housing Authority
replaced the high-rises with lower, more traditional housing, mostly
rowhouses. To create a economically balanced community, some of the
new units were reserved for subsidized tenants, and others were made
available to market-rate tenants. Additional units were built in the surrounding neighborhood, some on lots that had stood empty during the
neighborhood's down years. Inga Saffron, Pulitzer Prize–winning architecture critic of the *Philadelphia Inquirer*, found that the results were a
big improvement and that safety increased enormously.[12]

The Expanding Center

Center City, 2.2 square miles of level land between the Delaware River on the east and the Schuylkill River on the west, encompasses Philadelphia's downtown business district and some of the city's oldest neighborhoods. In 1682, William Penn, as proprietor of the Pennsylvania colony, wanted to avoid re-creating the congested city of London. To that end, he and surveyor Thomas Holme laid out the original portion of Philadelphia on a simple gridiron.

Most blocks were specified to have a length of 396 feet, a fairly short dimension by recent US development standards, but one that benefited future residents. Short blocks encourage pedestrians; in neighborhoods where the blocks are short, there are frequent intersections, and people have many choices for how to reach a destination. At an average pace, it takes a person only about a minute and a half to walk a 396-foot block. The widths of Center City's blocks vary, with small streets, courts, and alleys that were inserted in many of the blocks during the eighteenth and nineteenth centuries reinforcing Philadelphia's human scale.

Penn saw himself as founding a "greene country towne," where freestanding houses would sit in the center of large lots, but instead, Center City filled in densely, with attached rows of buildings. The streets gained a sense of enclosure, the feel of an "outdoor room."

In the twentieth century, many neighborhoods just beyond Center City were inhabited by people who worked in manufacturing or on the waterfront. When factory and waterfront employment declined after World War II, northern neighborhoods such as Northern Liberties and neighborhoods below South Street lost much of their population. Eventually, the trend reversed, and these neighborhoods began to gain residents. In response, the Center City District introduced a new term in 2011—Greater Center City—to describe the 7.7-square-mile combination of the old central area and the northern and southern neighborhoods now aligned with it.[a] Greater Center City's northern boundary is Girard Avenue, approximately a mile north of Vine Street. The southern boundary is Tasker Street, about nine-tenths of a mile south of South Street.

Center City's population has grown to about 62,000, and Greater Center City's, increasing 13 percent in the eleven-year period ending in 2013, has risen to more than 178,000. Center City, as a regional economic hub, also

[a] "The Success of Downtown Living: Expanding the Boundaries of Center City," *Center City Developments*, a publication of the Center City District and Central Philadelphia Development Corp., Apr. 2002, pp. 4–5.

boasts more than 288,000 jobs and 33,500 sole proprietors and partners in professional service firms.[b] In 2016, Walk Score rated Philadelphia the fourth most walkable city and the fifth most bike- and transit-friendly city in the United States.[c]

The core's relatively high population density—more than 38 residents per acre in Center City and as many as 63 persons per acre around Rittenhouse Square—supports a growing array of restaurants, stores, and amenities. More than 300 cafes and restaurants offer sidewalk dining (up from none in the early 1990s). That is one reason downtown blocks are livelier in the evening than they had been. The population of the city as a whole declined for half a century, reaching a low of 1,488,000 in 2006, but has since been growing, reaching 1,567,000 in 2015.

Public places attract people if there are congenial spots for sitting (or standing). Individuals will make seats of any surface that feels right. This scene is in Rittenhouse Square, originally called Southwest Square. (Photo by Philip Langdon)

---

[b] *State of Center City Philadelphia 2014* (Philadelphia: Center City District and Central Philadelphia Development Corp., 2014), pp. 5, 7, 11, 33, 47, 51.

[c] WalkScore, 2016 City & Neighborhood Ranking, accessed Nov. 29, 2016, https://www.walkscore.com/cities-and-neighborhoods/.

These modern townhouses in Center City have large areas of glass and decorative minibalconies that give a residential street a bit of a sense of habitation. Those pluses are offset, though, by a series of garage doors, making the block an unsatisfying place for pedestrians. (Photo by Philip Langdon)

Two Faces of Community Development

Because city government does not have the money and skill to address all Philadelphia's problems, much initiative has had to come from neighborhood organizations, foundations, and volunteer groups. In every part of Greater Center City, groups have gotten together to tackle concerns such as schools, safety, and parks.

Northern Liberties, a two-thirds-of-a-square-mile area northeast of Center City, is one neighborhood where volunteers have taken on

Map of Northern Liberties, indicating a few key features. (Drawing by Dhiru A. Thadani)

decrepit industrial properties and a lack of parks. The Northern Liberties Action Committee, a subgroup of the Northern Liberties Neighbors Association, was formed in 1994 to accept the donation of two acres that had been occupied by a tannery and a record-manufacturing plant. The aim was for the Neighbors Association to renovate the buildings and give them new uses. Before the plan could be acted on, however, the city condemned the buildings and knocked them down. The neighborhood was left with rubble-strewn land, and city taxpayers were left with more than $1 million in liens from the costs of demolition and from taxes unpaid by the now-gone industrial owners.

It might have been a disaster except for neighbors' persistence. An artist, Dennis Haugh, suggested converting the land into a park. Another resident, Jesse Gardner, organized volunteers and produced the park's design. Northern Liberties, described by longtime resident Janet Finegar as a liberal, funky community "one step out of the hippie culture," was the only zip code in Philadelphia with no public park. Residents wanted green space and recreational areas they could walk to.

With a grant from the Philadelphia Urban Resources Project and donations of money, services, and labor from neighbors, the park came into being in 1997. The volunteers named it Liberty Lands. They planted sixty trees during the first year of the park's existence, and they established community gardens. Later years brought more trees, picnic tables, an herb garden, a butterfly garden, a large lawn, and community events large and small. On the wall of a nearby building, Haugh painted "Cinema Verde," a mural that captured the evolution of the site from wilderness to factory to industrial wasteland and, finally, to community park.

In 1998, pressed by a local councilman, the city officially forgave the liens. Since then, the park has been owned free and clear by the Neighbors Association, which manages it. "It was very clear, at the time we were building it, that the park was bringing people together in a positive way," Finegar said. What makes the park crucial is that "it's a physical space," Finegar explained. "I think our neighborhood is incredibly unique; that's a bit nebulous, difficult to define. But I can take people to the park and they can see what we've built, and they might understand us better."

At Liberty Lands, and in probably every other community improvement effort in Philadelphia, contributions vary by individual. "It works in concentric circles," Finegar said. "There are five or six people who work five to ten hours a week on Liberty Lands. Then there is a group of twenty or thirty who are not there on as regular a basis, but who we can call on as needed. Then there are one hundred to two hundred who come out once or twice a year for a big work day, but who know the park really well and could be called on in an emergency."

Near Liberty Lands is a second new green space: Orianna Hill Park, which contains a community garden, a picnic area, and a large dog park ("one of the biggest and best in the city," according to Matt Ruben, president of the Neighbors Association). Orianna Hill is owned by a nonprofit organization that the neighbors established. It has more than six hundred members, and users of the park are asked to donate $50 a year.

Ruben, a Bryn Mawr professor who has lived since 2000 in an 1831 house on a street not quite 7 feet wide, has witnessed dramatic change during his time in the neighborhood. Northern Liberties' population, which he said peaked at about 17,000 in the 1930s, plummeted to about 3,500 by 1980 and leveled off, but then it jumped 60 percent between 2000 to 2010, showing the largest growth of any neighborhood in Philadelphia during that decade. Many people, some with an artistic bent, moved to Northern Liberties from nearby Old City when that neighborhood, a nightlife destination, became noisier and more expensive than it had been. With the influx of married families with children and students pursuing graduate degrees, Northern Liberties turned younger;

today, two of every five residents are twenty-five to thirty-four years old. Household income leaped to more than 50 percent above the city average. The white population more than doubled, and the proportion of African Americans declined.

Construction arrived in a big way. The development that brought Northern Liberties the most attention is the Piazza at Schmidt's, a sprawling seven-story mixed-use complex that Tower Investments opened in 2009 on North Second Street, where a Schmidt's brewery had stood. On the opposite side of the street is the Piazza's sister project: Liberties Walk, a three-story-high, four-block-long collection of apartments, stores, bars, and indoor and outdoor dining.

The Piazza features bold architecture arranged around an expansive open space. Many of the apartments have floor-to-ceiling walls of glass looking onto a plaza that has hosted rock concerts, flea markets, yoga festivals, and other events. Crowds have watched sports on the plaza's video screen and at other times reclined on chaise lounges, sunning themselves.

Tower prides itself on "transformational development" and asserts that the company made Northern Liberties "the place in Philadelphia, to live, work and play."[13] Certainly residents are grateful for the 52,000-square-foot Superfresh grocery store that Tower brought in. It is an amenity "no one ever thought we could have," Ruben said. The Piazza and Liberties Walk attracted commerce and activity to an area pockmarked with vacant, run-down buildings. "The whole idea," said Bart Blatstein, Tower Investments' CEO, "was to create a 5-minute community" boasting so many elements—including a dozen restaurants, a swim club in a converted machine shop, and retailers like Creep Records (a record store and head shop)—that "you never have to leave." When people do leave, it is less than a 5-minute walk to the Girard Station, where they can catch an elevated train, a trolley, or a bus. Many credit Blatstein's development with spurring other developers to build nearby.

The opening of Standard Tap on North Second Street at Poplar Street is credited with much of the rejuvenation of Northern Liberties. (Drawing by Dhiru A. Thadani)

Some people have qualms about the project, however. Neighborhood residents like Ruben have been unhappy with the development's haphazard retail mix and a "massive turnover" of stores. After initially offering discounted rents to creative retailers, Tower later filled those spaces with stores that could pay much more, a strategy that undermined the development's community orientation.[14] Tenants in the Piazza's apartments complained about indifferent building maintenance and management.

The commercial offerings suffered, Ruben said, from an emphasis on "alcohol first, food second, and restaurants that were just giant bars.

Everything else winds up moving toward that model." In 2013, the Piazza was sold to the Kushner Companies. Most of the public events eventually were discontinued, causing a commentator for *Hidden City Philadelphia* to complain that "today the Piazza's public space is chronically underused, leaving visitors feeling more like lone trespassers than participants in a vibrant community."[15] Consequently, in 2016, Kushner renamed the complex the Schmidt's Commons and promised a different mix of events, some of them more family-oriented.[16]

How surprising is it that a project as big as the Piazza at Schmidt's would leave many people dissatisfied? "Transformational projects" aimed at radically reshaping neighborhoods and revolutionizing their images

The central public space in Tower Investments' Piazza at Schmidt's development on North Second Street was touted as a dynamic gathering place in the Northern Liberties neighborhood. When big events are not being held there, it mostly feels lifeless. (Photo by Philip Langdon)

have been launched in countless US cities since the 1950s. Sometimes they have succeeded, but often they have succumbed to what Ruben calls "a monoculture," to being "dominated by a certain vibe." Run-down areas do need new energy, but in most cases, a better strategy is to work in a more organic fashion, with smaller increments of develop-ment and with close attention to neighborhood context.

Examples of that organic approach are not hard to find. The busi-ness that symbolizes and helped kick-start the entire Northern Liberties renaissance, said Ruben, is Standard Tap, a beloved tavern at Second and Poplar Streets, a few blocks south of the Piazza. It officially launched on New Year's Eve 1999. The founders, William Reed and Paul Kimport, fixed up a building on a prominent corner that had housed a tavern as far back as 1850 but that was sitting vacant and water-damaged in the late 1990s and was missing part of its roof. "That's why we could afford it," Reed told journalist Dayna Henninger.[17] He and Kimport decided to feature strictly local draft beers, starting with twelve taps. They produced seasonal dishes, using ingredients from the region, and they abstained from the usual bar accompaniments, such as TV screens. "We didn't want it to be an Irish pub or a British pub or a Belgian pub," Reed said. "We wanted it to be a Philadelphia pub." Ruben said that Standard Tap "helped start the trend that's now made gastropubs a sta-ble of drinking and dining across American cities."

After Standard Tap, other entrepreneurs arrived, and within about two years, development snowballed. The neighborhood filled with restaurants, cafes, and residences. The downside was that Northern Liberties' surging popularity caused property prices to jump, making it nearly impossible for Reed and Kimport to embark on new ventures there. "So we decided to look in Fishtown," the adjoining neighborhood to the northeast, Reed said. In 2004, they bought a bar called Johnny Brenda's on a prominent corner and turned it into a tavern, restaurant, and music venue that has a big following. In the years since, a number of small storefronts in Fishtown have been filled by new enterprises that fit well with the area. Little corner coffeehouses like ReAnimator have given quiet portions of the neighborhood new gathering places.

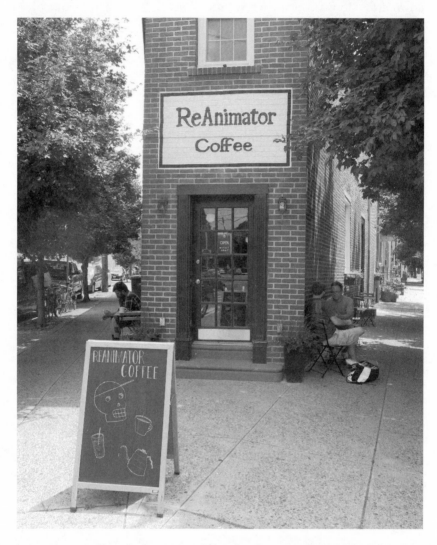

ReAnimator Coffee, which occupies the wedge-shaped end of an old brick building in Fishtown, is one of the many walk-to gathering places that are heightening the sociability of Philadelphia neighborhoods. (Photo by Philip Langdon)

Northern Liberties illustrates two contrasting ways of doing things, two faces of development. One is big projects built by centralized private capital, epitomized by the Piazza at Schmidt's. The other is smaller, patient undertakings, some of them the work of entrepreneurs, others the work of the community itself; a chief specimen is Liberty Lands. This second face of development usually is what makes a neighborhood deeply satisfying. It is possible that in some neighborhoods, even organic development may eventually lead to a torrent of development. "No matter what, communities don't stay the same," Finegar acknowledged, but, she pointed out, with organic development, "at least the community feels that what's happening is their own doing."

Critical to Northern Liberties' success is civic-minded people who have moved to the neighborhood and pitched in, year in and year out. Ruben said of the Neighbors Association, "We kind of do everything that we can," including planting trees and taking responsibility for sidewalk and curbside cleaning. "We do some of the functions that government doesn't do any more." The association acts as an information hub for residents and provides a venue for community members to voice their opinions on zoning and development issues.

Northern Liberties behaves, Ruben said, like an "urban village," a place where people know one another and walk to many of the things they need. It is close to Center City but benefits from being just far enough away from the downtown hubbub. "Everybody knows everybody," Ruben said. People are settling in places like Northern Liberties "because they're walkable," he observed. "The walkability is a huge thing."

The Rise of East Passyunk

Less than 2 miles south of Northern Liberties is another area—the East Passyunk Avenue commercial corridor—that has undergone a metamorphosis. East Passyunk (pronounced "pashunk"), a neighborhood that lost much of its vitality in the 1980s and 1990s, when many of its Italian American residents moved to New Jersey or elsewhere, has become a regional dining destination and a magnet for new residents, many of them young.

For decades, the avenue, which cuts diagonally across the city's grid, was known for two famous South Philadelphia cheesesteak rivals: Geno's Steaks and Pat's King of Steaks. The cheesesteak emporiums are still there, in all their neon glory, and so are pizzerias and old-style Italian eateries, but now, very conspicuously, the avenue also has a higher culinary level.

The restaurant renaissance began in 2005 when Lynn Rinaldi opened a white-tablecloth establishment emphasizing regional Italian fare made with ultrafresh ingredients. Rinaldi had grown up in this neighborhood of rowhouses mostly two stories high, 14 feet wide, and 32 feet deep, and she learned her trade by operating a cafe at the Pennsylvania Academy of Fine Arts and attending a local restaurant school. Upon getting hold of a former furniture store on East Passyunk near Tasker Street, she renovated it with help from her father, Dan Rinaldi, and converted it into a smart restaurant called Paradiso.[18] "We grow a significant amount of what we prepare," she told anyone who might be interested. "We have a garden on our roof."

In 2009, Lynn Rinaldi and her husband, Corey Baver, opened a second restaurant—a contemporary Japanese place called Izumi—half a block away. The two establishments gave other ambitious restaurateurs confidence to set up in the area, propelling the avenue into the upper ranks of Philadelphia dining destinations. "Top chefs are coming here," said Sam Sherman, who directed the nonprofit Passyunk Avenue Revitalization Corporation until 2016.

Celebrated restaurants can put a neighborhood on the map, but other businesses can also play major roles. "It would be a mistake to forget the importance of bars and coffeehouses in drawing people in their twenties to an area," said David Goldfarb, who arrived in the East

Passyunk area in 2005 when he was twenty-four. "Bars are interspersed throughout almost all our residential walkable neighborhoods." Bars are often more effective than restaurants at attracting lots of customers from the immediate neighborhood. Depending on how they are managed, they can infuse new life into their surroundings. In that sense, they are like coffeehouses and are extremely local. Two of the important bars for East Passyunk are Cantina Los Caballitos, which opened about the same time as Paradiso, and the Pub on Passyunk East, which opened a year later.

Goldfarb summed up the advantages of a neighborhood like East Passyunk this way:

> Living in a dense environment means a less stressful and time-consuming commute to work without the aid of a car. It's about a greater sense of community and partnership that naturally develops when you walk through a place and casually collide with neighbors. It's about feeling a sense of attachment to stores and bars and restaurants and their owners and employees. Frequently I will stop in to say a hello at a restaurant or store even if I'm not shopping or eating. It's about using a compact life to reduce environmental impact. For me, it boils down to this: a place you walk through is a place you know and love.

About wooing the woman who would become his wife, he said, "It's hard to imagine our courtship without hanging out in and walking to the coffeeshops, bars, restaurants, and other places that made up our early dating years."

Some might think that bars and coffeeshops would be less needed now that many people find potential romantic partners on the Internet. That is not so, according to Goldfarb. "Since online dating generates more first dates with people you may or may not have a spark with, having casual and convenient places to meet becomes important," he explained. Neighborhood hangouts are places where near-strangers can get acquainted face-to-face.

He pointed out another reason millennials like to live in neighborhoods where bars and taverns are within walking distance. "Among millennials, drunken driving has become so socially unacceptable," he said.

The flourishing of restaurants and retail establishments has been facilitated by the nonprofit Passyunk Avenue Revitalization Corporation (PARC), which buys vacant buildings, renovates them, and manages them for the long term, filling their ground floors with restaurants, stores, and other businesses. Upper floors, some of which languished as storage areas, have been redone by PARC and rented out as apartments. PARC uses the revenue from the rental properties to invest in cleaning, green space improvements, graffiti removal, and special events.

PARC strives for a useful balance of businesses, a blend of not only restaurants and cafes but also services such as a neighborhood hardware store. Affordable long-term leases are offered to promising enterprises. Because PARC owns a critical mass of buildings, it can write leases that require stores to stay open in the evenings and through the weekend. One reason the neighborhood's retailers declined in the 1980s was that many of them closed early, a practice left over from a time when customers were housewives who shopped on weekday mornings and afternoons.[19] Being open on evenings and weekends is crucial to most businesses' success today.

At the triangle formed by East Passyunk Avenue, Tasker Street, and South Eleventh Street, PARC planted trees, installed new benches, and refurbished the Singing Fountain, so called because its speakers fill the air with Frank Sinatra songs. "Here you can find old men playing chess, young mothers nursing their babies, and the weekly Farmers' Market full of Amish," an admirer of the plaza posted on Yelp.[20] After sunset,

One of the retailers the Passyunk Area Revitalization Corporation encouraged to open in the neighborhood is 1540 Hardware, at the corner of East Passyunk Avenue and Cross Street. (Drawing by Dhiru A. Thadani)

the plaza remains active. Said Sherman, "I see eighty-year-old people sitting at the fountain at midnight."

Demand for parking—a challenge for restaurants—has been met by introducing flexible valet parking along several blocks of the avenue. A customer can drop a car at a restaurant and later pick it up at any of several convenient locations.

One thing East Passyunk teaches us is that a community-based organization possessing significant resources can not only turn a corridor around but can also ensure that basic neighborhood-serving businesses

The Singing Fountain, the principal feature of a square on East Passyunk Avenue. (Drawing by Dhiru A. Thadani)

are part of the revival. Other neighborhoods—in Philadelphia or elsewhere—could apply what has been learned in East Passyunk. The resources required are not minuscule, but just suppose that foundations, philanthropists, or governments stepped forward with seed money or suppose that states started channeling some their revenue from dubious enterprises such as casino gambling into neighborhood nonprofit development groups. That is an idea worth investigating.[21]

A Neighborhood for All

The neighborhood benefits from extensive transit connections, including a short subway trip to downtown. Dan Pohlig, who is in his thirties, commutes by bicycle, a 9-minute ride, much of it on bike lanes that were painted on the streets not long ago. "This neighborhood is among the highest in the country in percentage of people who commute by bike," he said. Kandace Gollomp, a physician married to David Gold-farb, commutes by bike or subway to Children's Hospital of Philadelphia from the 930-square-foot rowhouse that the couple bought near the Singing Fountain. She cited the restaurants, the "new energy," and a grocery store and other essentials within walking distance as reasons she moved to the neighborhood.

People in older age brackets are moving there, too. Ed and Pam Zenzola had lived in Hong Kong and Tokyo during Ed's career as an international business executive, and in retirement they had settled in Horsham, Pennsylvania. They had expected that having a greenhouse and spending time growing orchids in Horsham would be fulfilling. The upshot, said Pam, is that "we were bored out of our minds in the suburbs." One day, Ed walked through their 150-home development, saw only four other people, and concluded it was time to move to someplace livelier. Because a number of large houses have recently been constructed in the East Passyunk area, they were able to find a 3,400-square-foot semidetached house—big enough for entertaining—in a section called Passyunk Square.

The couple now walk to cultural destinations like the Kimmel Center for the Performing Arts on South Broad Street, and they walk frequently in their neighborhood, continually running into people they know. "I cannot go out of my house," Pam said, "without someone saying 'How's it going?'"

Old-time homeowners are selling their houses to young couples with children. The change is "pretty orderly," Sherman said. "We haven't had the drama of race and class play out as in other parts of Philadelphia." The newcomers are contributing. Pam Zenzola, freed from the tedium of Horsham, was elected president of the Passyunk Square Civic Association.

Dan Rinaldi, Lynn's father, now in his early eighties, looks at the neighborhood's trajectory and offers a benediction: "It's for the best. Before, it was all ethnic Italians. Now it's more diverse." Sherman thinks that because of long-term stagnation in most Americans' incomes, many more people will be settling in walkable neighborhoods. "We're not wealthy anymore," he said. "This is the future: living like people do in East Passyunk."

Medallion installed in the sidewalk on East Passyunk Avenue. (Drawing by Dhiru A. Thadani)

Southwest Center City

The northwest tip of what was traditionally "South Philadelphia" has experienced extraordinary ups and downs. The area—which stretches southward from South Street for about a dozen blocks between Broad Street and the Schuylkill River—is known today by three different names: Southwest Center City, Graduate Hospital (a nod to a hospital that functioned from 1916 to 2007), and South of South.

This neighborhood developed rapidly in the 1860s and 1870s, and by the end of the nineteenth century, it was filled with two-story working-class rowhouses, more luxurious three-story rowhouses, large single-family houses, and other dwellings. The variety of housing accommodated a full range of African American residents, from laborers to businesspeople, musicians, teachers, and doctors. Julian F. Abele, a black architect known for his work on designs for the Philadelphia Museum of Art and estates on the Main Line, lived on Christian Street, eight blocks below South Street. The pathbreaking singer Marian Anderson was born in the neighborhood in 1897.

The neighborhood had a stable population of about 27,000 in the 1930s, but after World War II, in the face of redlining and other burdens, the most prosperous African Americans began moving to more distant sections of the city or out of Philadelphia entirely. Municipal officials viewed the area as blighted, and in the early 1960s, the City Planning Commission decided to replace a 2.6-mile swathe of South Street with the Crosstown Expressway, a high-speed link in a network of freeways proposed to ring Center City.[22]

After years of contention, the Crosstown proposal died. The years of uncertainty, however, had worsened the decay in this corridor, which held a mix of stores, housing, medical facilities, and other buildings. As housing abandonment, unemployment, and crime all rose, the neighborhood's population plummeted by 1980 to a little more than 12,000. Many rowhouses were razed during this time.

Around 1980, a countertrend appeared: the white population began to grow. "Living in a diverse, cheap, gritty area appealed to many whites," said Andrew Dalzell, who worked as a community organizer for the South of South Neighborhood Association (SOSNA). In the mid-1990s, not long after graduating from Bryn Mawr, Jennifer Hurley, who is white, rented an apartment at Twenty-Second and Kater Streets, just below South Street. Life near Philadelphia's center attracted her, but there were risks. "It was dicey enough that I felt nervous walking around by myself after eight o'clock at night," Hurley recalled.

By the beginning of the twenty-first century, a resurgence of Center City "made the neighborhood increasingly attractive to young professionals," Dalzell wrote in his history of Southwest Center City. The African American slice of the neighborhood's population—91 percent in 1980—declined to 72 percent in 2000 and to 32 percent in 2010. For the first time in ninety years, Center City's overall population increased.[23]

Was this change "gentrification"? That word, traceable to the English term *gentry*, is an intellectual obstacle; it fundamentally mischaracterizes many of the Americans who are moving into old urban neighborhoods. Historically, in Britain, the gentry were landed proprietors who inherited wealth and social position and who saw themselves as superior to people who worked for a living. The gentry did not inhabit the very top of the social structure. Unlike dukes, earls, and others in the nobility, members of the gentry lacked hereditary titles and coats of arms, but they did possess something of great importance: country estates. Often the estates were so large or valuable that their owners had no need to support themselves, except through managing their own land. Many of the gentry lived entirely off rental income from tenant farms they controlled.

In US cities, the equivalent is hard to find. Those who are tagged gentrifiers do not they behave like masters of rural estates. Most of the

The Grays Ferry Triangle, where South Street, Twenty-Third Street, and Grays Ferry Avenue intersect, was redeveloped by the South of South Neighborhood Association into a popular gathering place. The association made sure that people were given the option of sitting "campfire style" around a historic fountain installed in 1901 for horses to quench their thirst. (Photo by Philip Langdon)

individuals and couples who buy homes in reviving neighborhoods must work to support themselves, often spending long hours at their jobs. Before they get started on their careers, it is not uncommon for them to complete many years of study. They are tech people, business executives, restaurant owners, chefs, doctors, nurses, assistant professors, architects, entrepreneurs, teachers, writers, artists, and so on. They do not, for the most part, take everything in ease. Gentrification is not a term that clarifies the urban situation.

A more useful term than gentrification is displacement, which looks at whether existing residents are being forced out and at who those residents are. Clearly, some low-income people leave when new residents with high incomes move into inexpensive places and bid up the price of housing. Southwest Center City is a place where we can examine what happens as the economy changes.

"It is common to hear people say that residents were 'pushed[,]' 'forced' or 'squeezed' out of their neighborhoods," Dalzell wrote in his history of Southwest Center City. "In some instances, this was indeed the case—median rents jumped from $283 in 1990 to nearly $1,000 in 2010. Home values and property taxes of some (but not all) have also risen. In other cases, predatory real estate practices hoodwinked the vulnerable." He noted, however, that "2010 Census data document a national trend of 'black flight' (like 'white flight' in the prior century) from urban centers to the suburbs and the South. Many could cash in on the newly inflated value of their old home and move to areas where many of their family and friends lived."

Murray Spencer, a black architect in his early sixties, has lived in the neighborhood since 1976, most of that time in a three-story rowhouse he bought on Christian Street across from the Christian Street YMCA, the first black YMCA in Philadelphia to have its own building. (A teenaged Wilt Chamberlain distinguished himself on the basketball court of that Y.) Spencer said that when he moved to Christian Street, "the block was 100 percent African American, the housing stock was about 75 percent rental, and it was in relatively good condition."

"I liked it a lot," he said. "I could walk or take a bus to [the University of Pennsylvania], across the South Street Bridge." Parts of Southwest Center City were suffering from gang violence, but not his section of Christian Street. There was one incident in which someone pulled a gun on Spencer and a cousin of his, but on the whole, he said, "I did not feel unsafe. If you were not in the wrong element, trouble didn't find you."

Nearby public schools were substandard, though, so Spencer and his wife sent one son to a Catholic school and the other to a better-performing public school near the neighborhood. In his professional life, Spencer has often designed houses for people who were living in Center City or in other city neighborhoods and who moved out when their children did not, as he put it, "'win the lottery' for placement in one of several public elementary schools with high or superior academics." Among African Americans moving out, he has seen two distinct patterns. First, older blacks have mainly gone south to join their grown children or have shifted to smaller homes that fit their retirement needs. Second, some of the lower-income blacks who rent have been moving to cheaper locales like Point Breeze, a neighborhood immediately to the south, which is a few years behind Southwest Center City in the cycle of revitalization and renovation.

Consequently, since about 2015, Spencer's block has become predominantly white and owner-occupied. Some of the rental properties have been converted to condominiums. "I paid $24,000 for my house," he said. "It's now worth just south of $300,000." The Edwin M. Stanton Elementary School on his block, whose enrollment is 85 percent African American, "has become a good school," Spencer observed. "A lot of the new people started sending their children there," he said, and parental involvement at Stanton has grown, which has boosted achievement. He pointed out that parents relatively new to the neighborhood raised money to supplement the school's budget and persuaded businesses to donate computers, initiatives that have benefited blacks as well as whites. "In my neighborhood, unlike the city as a whole, people are generally happy with the schools," Spencer said.

In 2013, Dalzell wrote that "crime is down, and violent crime is exceedingly rare." He described Southwest Center City as "vibrant, convivial, and community-minded." New residents move there for

Passersby inspect Philadelphia's Magic Gardens on South Street, where Isaiah Zagar fashioned bicycle wheels, colored bottles, handmade tiles, and a multitude of other objects into the front wall of what is now a nonprofit art environment and community center. Through their art, Zagar and his wife, Julia, contributed to the "South Street Renaissance" and helped revive a corridor that the city once planned to knock down for an expressway. (Photo by Philip Langdon)

varied reasons, many of which involve walkability, convenience, and relative affordability.

On a summer evening in 2014, I stopped at a neighborhood association fund-raising dinner in the Grays Ferry Triangle, at the junction of South Street, Grays Ferry, and Twenty-Third Street. Mainly through SOSNA's efforts, the triangle has developed into a congenial outdoor gathering place. There a young woman, Jennifer Leupold, told me she was attracted to the neighborhood by "how accessible everything was. I've got a grocery store, liquor store, parks, entertainment," she said. "Within six to ten blocks is everything I need. My husband has a Vespa, and I have a bike. I bike all the time. That's my main form of transportation." Her husband, Jeff Leupold, a graphic designer who grew up outside the city, expressed satisfaction with being close to things, eliminating a long commute. "I did not want to sit in a car for an hour," he said, "or even in a train for that long."

Philadelphia has forty-two bus lines, five trolley lines, three subways, thirteen regional train lines, and Amtrak's Northeast corridor service, which together help explain why only 28 percent of Center City residents commute by car. Forty-four percent walk or bike to work, and another 20 percent use public transit.[24] Many people complain that buses do not come frequently enough or are overcrowded, but fortunately the bus is only one option. "I feel one reason this neighborhood has gentrified," said Inga Saffron, "is that instead of waiting 15 minutes for a SEPTA bus, you can bike there in 10 minutes and have total control." Biking engages riders in the city's environment, which is generally a plus, and on narrow streets, cars usually move slowly enough for cyclists to believe they are not in danger.

Brian Lawson, a cable company executive in his early fifties, told me that before he moved to Philadelphia to work at the headquarters of Comcast, he had lived in Dallas, Kansas City, and Miami—"big driving cities." He seized the opportunity to escape that style of life, first renting at Washington Square, a little more than a mile from Comcast, and then buying a house near Washington Avenue, Southwest Center City's southern boundary, about a mile and a half from his office. The house he bought was 1,200 square feet, less than half the size of the one he had in Kansas City.

Not everything has gone without a hitch. Early in his tenure, he said, "my house was broken into twice in six months." Trash strewn around the neighborhood bothered him, so, Lawson said, "I used to spend several hours each weekend picking up trash." Some of the people who had lived nearby for a long time chastised him for cleaning up. "The city is supposed to do that," they told him. The financially stressed city was not doing the cleaning, so he figured he would make things better himself. Where he saw that a trash can was needed, he supplied it. "Across the street is a block-long warehouse that sells industrial supplies," he told me. "I chained a trash can to a telephone pole on their property." As time went by, some longtime residents joined his cleanup campaign. "We got a broom for a ninety-year-old, and he's out sweeping the street and the sidewalk," Lawson said. "You just bite the bullet and make it better as much as you can."

The old rowdiness is not entirely gone. A man got angry at Lawson for calling the police when a fight indoors erupted onto the sidewalk. "It's still gritty," Lawson said of parts of the area. "The neighborhood across Washington Avenue, it's block by block." Close to him, however, four houses or lots that had stood vacant are now all occupied. "There are no vacant properties or abandoned lots anymore," he said.

In Lawson's view, personal involvement is crucial for turning a neglected area into a safe, walkable neighborhood; a new resident has to think about how to be effective. "When we first moved here, we said hello to everyone," he said. "We made eye contact." What happened to the ninety-year-old man with the broom? "'We gave him a freshly cooked Thanksgiving dinner," Lawson said. A woman in her late eighties looks to Lawson for help. "I've been paying her cable bill for the last six years," he said. "Now she doesn't knock on my door and say 'My TV isn't working.'"

"You really see the income disparity and how I grew up versus how kids here are brought up—which most people [in America] don't see," he continued. "It's a difficult discussion topic, but you really get to see it. I started treating people very differently. I was not the high-energy, corporate person on the go-go-go anymore. I take the time to listen. One kid wanted to go to community college. I helped him fill out the financial aid forms. It's a tough balancing act. You want to put yourself out there, but you don't want to go too far."

Lest Lawson's story be seen as suggesting that his life in Southwest Center City is mainly about sacrifice, he is quick to identify the advantages of the choice he made. "Things I like about the neighborhood: When you're walking down the street, you always run into people you know. We very rarely go to a grocery store. I stop into little shops between home and Comcast and bring home something for tonight," he said. "We go to the Italian Market," an old-time open-air market in a neighborhood not far to the east. "I walk to work every day. I haven't driven a car in eight years."

Another day, I met the *Philadelphia Inquirer*'s Saffron at the Grays Ferry Triangle and walked south with her, looking at narrow streets of mostly two- and three-story rowhouses. When we passed African American residents sitting on stoops or relaxing in front of their homes, many of them greeted us. "Philadelphia is very neighborhood-oriented," Saffron remarked, and blacks, especially, tend to say hello to people passing by, including strangers. Many millennials do not offer greetings on the street, and their failure to do so is, for some blacks, a source of friction.

Looked at another way, the millennials' obliviousness is a sign of how racial strain has eased. "We're getting over some of our issues about race," Saffron said, pointing out that unlike previous generations, "millennials are not aware of tension over race." Racial fears and antagonisms underlay much of the city's decay. Although the friction has not disappeared, it has receded, which has allowed the intrinsic appeal of urban living to reemerge with great strength. It is possible that the widely reported killings of blacks by police across the United States and the rise of the Black Lives Matter campaign may usher in renewed antagonism, but so far, tension has remained much less than it was in the 1960s.

Newcomers have joined organizations to improve the Southwest Center City neighborhood. Jennifer Leupold cited a number of projects launched by SOSNA or other groups. She said, "The association does a monthly cleanup. We did crowdsourcing for trash containers on a corner. We've done a lot of surveying to find out where most of the trash is. There are two K-to-8 schools where kids are required to do community services. We give them trash-grabbers."

Ivy Olesh and her husband, Matt, attracted by the neighborhood's diversity, easy access to Center City, and closeness to parks like the Schuylkill River Trail, bought a newly built townhouse in Southwest Center City in 2007. "We quickly saw that our neighbors were involved in helping to keep the neighborhood a great place and wanted to do more, and that made us excited," she said. Within months, the Oleshes started a volunteer group that has planted more than three hundred trees. In 2009 and 2010, they started Friends of Chester Arthur (FOCA), a volunteer group that helps Chester A. Arthur School. This predominantly low-income public school on Catharine Street serves kindergarten through eighth-grade students, 72 percent of whom are African American. FOCA organized daily tutoring at the school, supported afterschool clubs, and convinced Olin, one of the city's leading landscape architecture firms, to develop a conceptual master plan for the playground at no charge.[25] FOCA then paid Salt Design Studio to carry the master plan into construction.

Recognizing that the Philadelphia school system was strapped for resources, the volunteers mobilized and raised $1.7 million from a variety of sources—among them the William Penn Foundation, the Philadelphia Water Department, Wells Fargo, and the community itself—for a panoply of improvements to the school's grounds, including a first-of-its-kind outdoor space for teaching science, technology, engineering, and mathematics. Groundbreaking for the biggest part of the project took place in July 2016.

"A lot of new families have really gotten behind the schools," said Abby Rambo, SOSNA's executive director. "They want their kids to

A playground at Chester A. Arthur School in Southwest Center City is being turned into an outdoor space for teaching science, technology, engineering, and mathematics thanks to fund-raising led by the Friends of Chester Arthur. In this photo of the July 2016 groundbreaking ceremony, Ivy Olesh, president of the volunteer group, is third from right, and Mike Burlando, cochair of the group's schoolyard committee, is on the far right. (Photo courtesy of Friends of Chester Arthur)

go to public schools in the neighborhood, not far away." Many parents join FOCA before their children are old enough for kindergarten. That was the case with the Oleshes. Their son Brody entered kindergarten at Chester Arthur in the fall of 2016.

Through SOSNA, small parks and play areas have been created in the neighborhood. Initiatives like those benefit people of all races and income levels. Among African Americans, there is some resentment because as whites with higher incomes have moved in, many rental properties have been converted to homeownership, and rents have escalated. "Often the policies we work on are more for homeowners than renters," said Ivelisse Cruz, SOSNA's youngest board member, who is of black and Puerto Rican lineage. Cruz hopes to represent the rental population within the organization and help ease the friction. "I am trying to do more outreach," she said. "I am trying to bridge the gap."

Contending Attitudes

The biggest divide in Philadelphia these days may not be over race; it may be over the shaping of buildings, blocks, and neighborhoods to support a walkable way of life and over change itself. Greater Center City has moved steadily toward compact, relatively dense living, connected by walking, biking, and public transit. The advantages of this healthy, low-pollution mode of living become more obvious every year as the effects of climate change, obesity, and physical inactivity gain attention, yet it is impossible to talk to a range of Philadelphians without hearing about conflict over parking, building heights, and mixing of uses.

Many older people, accustomed to driving and owning cars, still believe that plentiful parking is absolutely necessary on their own block and on most of the blocks they visit. They oppose development that does not include plenty of off-street parking. Younger people in Greater Center City generally understand that to make a walkable community, you have to deemphasize garages: build fewer of them and place them where they will do the least damage to the atmosphere of the streets and sidewalks. These residents recognize that a line of garage doors on the front of a group of townhouses deadens the street. When younger people and urban designers call for reducing the volume of parking in new residential development, older people protest, fearing that their

Sidewalk dining, as shown here at Spruce and South Twentieth Streets, has blossomed as Center City has grown safer and has in turn reinforced the hospitable quality of many neighborhood streets. Next to the curb is a bike lane. (Photo by Philip Langdon)

own blocks will get parked up. Or, Ed Zenzola suggested, they protest because fundamentally they fear change.

In Southwest Center City, the more contemporary thinkers proposed allowing modestly taller buildings to be constructed on vacant land just west of the Grays Ferry Triangle. This conspicuous intersection was a logical spot for building a story or two higher. If a city is going to meet the growing demand for walkable neighborhoods by building slightly higher, it is better to do so at intersections rather than haphazardly here and there. Some of the older residents, however, objected and ultimately prevented the rise in height at the triangle.

In Southwest Center City, as in other neighborhoods, the new thinking recognizes that gathering places foster neighborhood connectedness, but not all residents share that thinking. For example, younger residents favored allowing sidewalk dining outside Sidecar, a once-raucous tavern that had become quieter and more orderly in recent years. Old-time residents, however, knew the tavern from its disruptive days and seemed to think that if Sidecar had once been a source of trouble, it would be a source of trouble forever. They opposed sidewalk dining.

What will likely happen is that resistance to valid urban propositions will gradually diminish. As Greater Center City becomes more walkable, safe, and convivial, the advantages of a pedestrian-oriented urban setting will win over more of the doubters. The younger generation will be the victors. "You've got a whole generation that wants to be here," said Paul Levy of the Center City District. "People in their late teens and twenties pride themselves on sustainable living. They want to bike, not have a car. You don't need a car to live in the city. It is a huge cultural change." He concluded, "This is long beyond a fad."

Physical changes—parks, gathering places, mixed-use development, sometimes taller buildings—will have to be introduced into more and more neighborhoods. Many people would like to live in or near Center City but are deterred by the rise in real estate prices. Chief reasons that neighborhoods on the edges of Center City have attracted so much energy and enthusiasm are that they have certain basic things right— such as the relationship of buildings to streets—and they are cheaper than Center City. People looking for walkable environments have shown a willingness to settle a little farther out. Observes Hurley, "I can plot where my friends bought houses by when they bought them." The later her friends bought, the farther out they live.

The tactics that have enlivened Northern Liberties, East Passyunk, and Southwest Center City need to be applied to additional neighborhoods

that possess a sound basic structure. Keeping Greater Center City affordable will depend, to a large degree, on making other neighborhoods in
other parts of the city as livable as the center has become.

ONE STOP MART & DELI
CAFFE BRAVO
ROMEO & CESARE'S
EAST ROCK PHARMACY
ORANGE STREET MARKET
EAST ROCK COFFEE
NICA'S MARKET
CAFE ROMEO

PROSPECT ST.
EAST ROCK PARK
COTTAGE ST.
WILLOW ST.
WHITNEY AVE
5 MIN. WALK
ORANGE ST.
EDWARDS ST.
STATE ST.
ELM ST.
GREEN
COLLEGE ST.
CHURCH ST.
CHAPEL ST.

Map of the downtown and East Rock sections of New Haven. The shaded area near the bottom of the map indicates the original nine squares laid out by the founding Puritans in 1638, centering on the Green. The shaded area above that is East Rock, which developed in the nineteenth and early twentieth centuries. (Drawing by Dhiru A. Thadani)

CHAPTER 2

Creating Gathering Places:
The East Rock Neighborhood,
New Haven, Connecticut

Since the early 1980s, my wife and I have lived in East Rock, a New Haven neighborhood that discovered ways to create the "third places" advocated by Ray Oldenburg in his illuminating book, *The Great Good Place: Cafes, Coffee Shops, Community Centers, Beauty Parlors, General Stores, Bars, Hangouts, and How They Get You Through the Day.* Oldenburg, a sociologist at the University of West Florida, had grown dissatisfied with daily life in his Pensacola neighborhood during the 1970s, and that led him to wonder whether people were feeling the same frustrations in other communities across the United States. In the book that resulted, published in 1989, he concluded that "for some time now, the course of urban growth and development in the United States has been hostile to an informal public life; we are failing to provide either suitable or sufficient gathering places necessary for it."[1]

Oldenburg argued that Americans needed, and largely lacked, places where they could find relief from the stresses encountered in the two principal sites of daily life: home and the workplace. Third places—informal gathering places—were essential, he said, and they should be within walking distance of home or work so that people can easily integrate them into their everyday routines.

This chapter looks at how the people of East Rock responded to this need. By overcoming various obstacles, they were able to create a series of congenial gathering places within walking distance of many residents' homes.

Getting Around

When we moved to East Rock in 1983, several things attracted us. First, the location was close to downtown and Yale University, which meant I could sometimes walk—but more often bike—to well-stocked libraries, free lectures, and many other public events. I could leave the car at home.

Second, East Rock offered an abundance of well-crafted houses from the late nineteenth and early twentieth centuries. Each single-family, two-family, or three-family dwelling stood on its own lot, but the houses were close enough together that people had many opportunities to see and get to know their neighbors. Mixed in among the houses were apartment buildings that generally had a domestic scale; rarely more than three stories high, they had proportions and materials echoing those of the houses. Physically, the buildings in East Rock fit together.

Third, the neighborhood had a convenient network of streets and sidewalks, lined by oaks, maples, and other shade trees, that made for pleasurable walking. In every direction, there was a choice of routes, with rarely a dead end. It was the opposite of modern suburbs, where cul-de-sacs, meant to eliminate the dangers of through traffic, make every trip longer and more circuitous than it need be. To me, East Rock—1 square mile with 9,100 inhabitants, running from the northern edge of downtown to the southern border of suburban Hamden—was a welcoming

House with an elaborately decorated porch overlooking Canner Street. Porches are prominent on many one-, two-, and three-family houses in East Rock. (Photo by Philip Langdon)

landscape, level for the most part but with a ridge called Prospect Hill forming its western flank.[2]

When neighbors wanted more challenging terrain, they hiked the steep trails of East Rock Park, a 400-acre-plus expanse of marshes, meadows, woodlands, and cliffs on the neighborhood's northern edge. The cliffs of trap rock, a volcanic rock containing iron, rose almost straight up for 340 feet from the winding Mill River at their base. In overcast weather, the cliffs were rust-colored, but in summer sun, they glowed reddish-orange; they looked like the backdrop of a Western film by John Ford.

We wanted a neighborhood that was pleasurable to explore on foot, and East Rock certainly was that. On some blocks, there were sumptuous architect-designed houses in Queen Anne, Arts and Crafts, Colonial

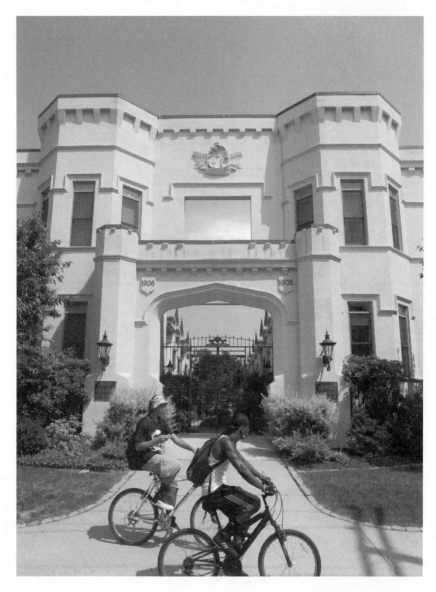

The facade of a 1906–1908 armory on Orange Street was saved and now serves as the entrance to two rows of apartments immediately behind. (Photo by Philip Langdon)

This porch—really just a platform—on Autumn Street shows both how close a raised sitting area can come to the sidewalk and how minimal its construction can be. Enjoying it are Anton Bures, Jenya Weinreb, and their son, Leo Bures Weinreb. (Photo by Philip Langdon)

Revival, Gothic Revival, and other historical styles, gratifying to look at, whether for the first time or the hundredth. On other blocks, two- and three-family houses predominated; they were plainer, but many had front porches stacked two or three high, which created an atmosphere of welcome. Garages were nearly always at the backs of the lots, not intruding on the streetscape.

Still other blocks were lined with old, narrow cottages built for working-class residents. On some of those blocks, there was a brief gap where one cottage sat far to the back of its lot, behind a lawn 60 feet deep, instead of being close to the street like all the others. That con- trast—a kind of breathing space in the block—punctuated an otherwise rigorous row and was one of the many charming quirks of East Rock.

Some East Rock blocks were approximately 400 to 600 feet long, which is manageable for people getting around on foot. Others were in the 700- to 900-foot range, which is not as good because longer blocks mean a smaller choice of routes. A couple of streets, Livingston and Everit, had blocks that stretched on for more than a third of a mile. From a pedestrian's perspective, that would ordinarily be a problem, but those two 1,900-foot blocks had such beautiful early-twentieth-century houses that I rarely minded the length.

Because the neighborhood developed before modern, separate-use zoning, many nonresidential uses were sprinkled throughout: schools, offices, day care centers, doctors, dentists, laundries, dry cleaners, hair cutters, beauticians, taverns (on the less upscale blocks), and at least fifteen churches. There were useful destinations for people to walk to.

The Stores of Orange Street

On East Rock's eastern edge, State Street was a commercial corridor known in the 1980s for stores selling secondhand furniture. Since then, the used-furniture stores have all closed or moved, and State Street has become a strip with small stores of many kinds, restaurants, bars, a state

This generously ornamented house on Whitney Avenue is one of the many grand houses built in East Rock around the turn of the twentieth century and since converted to other uses. It is now the Whitney Arts Center, used for everything from ballet classes to church gatherings. (Photo by Philip Langdon)

probation office, a health clinic, the headquarters of the New Haven Preservation Trust, and apartments.

For most East Rock residents, the retail corridor that matters is Orange Street, which runs straight through the center of the neighborhood,

A New Haven triple-decker with stacked front porches helps keep activity on
Eagle Street in East Rock under the eyes of residents. (Photo by Philip Langdon)

from downtown to the base of the cliffs. Grocery and convenience stores, most of them owned by people whose parents or grandparents had come to New Haven from Italy, squeezed in between Orange Street's houses and apartment buildings. By the 1980s, many of the stores had been there for years.

At the Orange Food Mart, the butcher shop run by Jimmy Apuzzo attracted a steady clientele. At the tiny DeRose's Market, the voluble, rotund Pete DeRose stocked high-quality cheeses, crusty European breads, and other specialty items that were not available in most New Haven stores at the time. Customers came not just from East Rock but from a wide area for the olive oils, Meyer lemons, and other products he offered.

The Prime Market, run by the compact, extroverted Nick Casella, was the busiest store on the street. The shop's four narrow aisles, stacked high with merchandise, were jammed with customers. Toward the rear of the store, a knot of people waited their turn at the butcher department. Prices generally were not cheap, but each week Casella advertised a few staples that matched or beat the suburban supermarkets.

The Prime Market's off-street parking was of the token variety: just three spaces on the asphalt pavement in front of the entrance. Stores on Orange Street were not big on parking; at most of them, customers who came by car had to park on the street, between bus stops and residential driveways. The customers continued coming nonetheless, one way or another. Older women from the more working--class eastern side of the neighborhood wheeled lightweight metal carts up and down Orange Street and then trundled home with their cooking ingredients for the next few days. Younger customers stuffed their purchases into backpacks. I bought a bicycle with two metal baskets on the rear; it is amazing how many groceries can be carried on a bike.

Romeo & Cesare's Gourmet Shop was the first of Orange Street's Italian grocery and take-out stores to add a plaza out front for customers. Today, seven outdoor dining and gathering places operate within a span of several blocks, adding sociability to the corridor. (Photo by Philip Langdon)

Casella posted a motto by the entrance: "Not just a grocery store but a social institution." It captured something about the store: when customers went to the Prime, they ran into people they knew.

The bigger reality, however, was that East Rock did not offer many places where people of all kinds, no matter their social class, employment, education, or income, could hang out. Such places were greatly needed, in part to alleviate New Haven's ingrained social divisions.

New Haven had been a diversified industrial center from the late nineteenth century through the 1950s, but after that, manufacturing petered out. The decline of industries such as gun making, lock making, and clock manufacturing was offset to some extent by the growth of Yale. By the 1980s, Yale had become the keystone of the local economy, but it was an elite private institution, given to intense status-consciousness. Perhaps a select number of Yale faculty and administrators felt secure, but the university's hierarchy contained myriad subtle gradations, and it was easy—in fact, normal—for people to be put on the defensive by Yale's culture of constant comparison. If you were not affiliated with Yale, you might wonder, "Am I a nobody?"

Will Baker, a non-Yalie who worked in New Haven from 2004 to 2014—first for a rare-book dealer and then as director of the Institute Library, a membership library founded in 1826—told me that when he was on or near the campus, he sometimes had "a sense of being invisible or not counting." On streets like Whitney Avenue, which connects Yale and downtown to East Rock, he detected "a level of anxiety" in the air. For Baker, the feeling of not having achieved much would arise, for instance, when a graduate student whooshed past on a bicycle on the sidewalk, nearly clipping him. On Whitney, Baker observed, it was as if "everyone had blinders on."

East Rock was susceptible to this uneasiness because many of the neighborhood's homeowners were Yale professors and staff members and many of the renters were graduate students or rank-and-file university employees. There were a few public places in East Rock where residents could get together. Those who owned dogs (and there were lots of them) had conversations and bonded with one another when they took their dogs to East Rock Park or Edgerton Park, a smaller park on a former estate behind gray stone walls on Whitney Avenue. Churchgoers could gather with their coreligionists in the neighborhood's houses of worship. Well-off families might join the Lawn Club, an organization with dining rooms, ballroom, tennis courts, and a pool. East Rock also offered a few taverns, including one so reclusive that until recently it did not even post a name on its exterior. These spots did not answer the needs of everyone. New Haven needed more third places that were out in open.

Return of the Drugstore

In June 2011, after 102 years in the ground floor of a red brick apartment building at Orange and Linden Streets, the Hall-Benedict Drug Company shut down. The closing was a double loss for the neighborhood. Besides having been East Rock's last surviving pharmacy, Hall-Benedict had operated a contract post office, the only place in the neighborhood where people could buy stamps, mail packages, and obtain other postal services.

Although chain drugstores and in-supermarket pharmacies have driven most of America's independent drugstores out of business since the 1980s, East Rock residents hoped that somehow their corner drugstore would be revived. The building's owners thought that idea was feasible, too, and got in touch with a company that helps independent Connecticut drugstores handle paperwork between pharmacies and government agencies. By that route, they found Connecticut Pharmacy, a business group that operated a drugstore in Norwalk, Connecticut, and was eager to expand.

Connecticut Pharmacy renovated the store and in September 2011 reopened it as East Rock Pharmacy. Soon it was doing business sixty hours each workweek, eight hours on Saturday, and six hours on Sunday. It also was on call around the clock. "Any emergency, we pick up the phone," said Ka Wa Chan, a pharmacist and partner in the company. "Sometimes a customer telephones and says he can't make it to the store till 7:15. I tell him, 'We're here.'" Chan would then stay late.

"I used to work with a chain for fifteen years," said Chan, who grew up in Hong Kong and attended pharmacy school in New York. "A pharmacy in a big chain," he said, "is more like a factory." He switched to an independent in part because it is a more personal enterprise. Some pharmacists, he said, are keen to own, manage, or work in small or nonchain stores.

"We get to know the families very well," said Scott Wolak, Connecticut Pharmacy's managing partner. If a patient has chronic conditions, the pharmacist speaks to the caregiver monthly. "We speak with the doctors *and* the patients," he said. "We spend a lot of time on medication management."

"You survive in a different scale," Chan said of the economics of a neighborhood pharmacy. "If the volume is low, you can't hire as many people. At first, everybody was doing deliveries, including myself." Within three years of opening, the store had fully established itself, with fifteen employees.

Behind the counter, facing banks of computers, several workers file orders for nursing homes spread across dozens of miles of southern Connecticut. They pack each nursing home patient's medications into "planners" holding a week's worth of pills, arranged by day. This service to long-term care facilities, including hospices, helps make the store viable. "The only way to make it work these days is to do what the chains don't," said Wolak. "A while ago, we got a call from a hospice at 2:30 in the morning; they needed end-of-life medications." The store, which contracts with three independent drivers, delivered them despite the hour. Through a group-buying organization, the pharmacy is able to "offer better prices compared to the big chains on both products and prescription drugs," Chan said. "Independent pharmacies, that niche is growing."

Because the old store had a postal operation and customers relied on it, the new pharmacy reestablished the postal counter, even though it is not a moneymaking operation. If a customer buys stamps with a credit card, the store actually loses money, according to Chan. On the other hand, people who come to buy stamps or mail packages buy other things—a bottle of aspirin or a New Haven T-shirt or a children's book—while they are in the store.

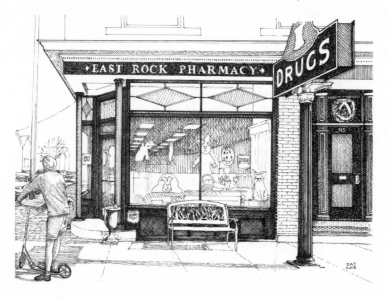

After the Hall-Benedict Drug Company closed in 2011, concluding 102 years at the corner of Orange and Linden Streets, a new pharmacy was enticed to open in its mixed-use, three-story building. To the neighborhood's delight, the new East Rock Pharmacy, which also runs a postal operation, has thrived. (Drawing by Dhiru A. Thadani)

The Coming of the Cafes

To fill the gap, what was needed was an entrepreneur intent on providing people with a place to linger and talk. The need was first filled by Louise "Lulu" deCarrone, an assertive young woman who had lost her job in a law firm. In April 1991, around the corner from the Orange Food Mart and the Orange Liquor Store, deCarrone opened Lulu European Coffeehouse. She strived to make it sociable.

Lulu's was tiny—"25 feet wide and 10 feet deep," deCarrone recollected when I interviewed her years later. The space, once occupied by a shoe repair shop but vacant in the early 1990s, was big enough for coffee-brewing equipment, a pastry case 5 feet wide and almost 5 feet high, two round tables for customers, and not much more. People were welcome to spend time there, but they would have to share the tables with whoever came in, friend or stranger. The compactness was dictated by deCarrone's tight finances—she was a single mother who started the business with $500 of her savings—but the size also fit her intentions. DeCarrone liked to keep people close; she wanted to talk with them, and she wanted them to talk with one another.

Lulu's became a favorite place in the neighborhood for animated conversation. East Rock's representatives on the board of aldermen started holding regular hours at Lulu's; people would come to discuss what was happening in the neighborhood and the city. The location on Cottage Street, a street of closely spaced houses within sight of Orange Street, was convenient for people arriving on foot or bicycle.

As the clientele grew, deCarrone had another thought: "Why are we not sitting outside?" Outdoor seating would allow the shop to serve more customers. It would be even more of a gathering place. She raised the idea with a staff member in the New Haven City Plan Department and got nowhere. She recalled with incredulity what the city employee told her: "We don't want to promote opportunities for drive-by shootings." During the crack cocaine epidemic in the early 1990s, New

Haven was plagued with drive-by shootings. The shootings, however, were in rougher parts of the city and occasionally downtown, not in East Rock.

In March, even before the winter snow disappears, East Rock residents begin repopulating the Orange Street plazas. These businesses are at the corner of Orange and Cottage Streets. (Photo by Philip Langdon)

An employee in the city's business development office also was dismissive, she said, telling her, "You don't belong in East Rock. You are taking the shine away from Chapel Street," the principal downtown retail street, which was not doing well at the time and sorely needed small businesses.

DeCarrone remained undeterred. It takes perseverance to change the outlook of a plodding municipal bureaucracy. She asked Alderman Cameron Staples to help persuade the City Plan Department that outdoor seating would not invite crime; on the contrary, it would make crime less likely because populated places are generally safer than places where people stay indoors.

DeCarrone received permission and repaired the broken patio outside the shop. "It cost $1,000 to have the cement poured. I remember saving up for it," she recalled. "I had an awning made. It gave me a nice

---

Can We Talk?

One day in 2007, Lulu deCarrone looked over her coffeehouse on Cottage Street. "The store was like a crypt, and it dawned on me that I hate it," she recalled. "It felt like an office." Most of the tables were occupied by people on computers. "Two older ladies walked in who hadn't seen each other in along time. They were having a great time," she said, but their talk annoyed the laptop people, who started saying "shhhh" and glaring at the offenders.

By the next day, deCarrone had decided what she would do: she posted a sign banning the use of laptops. Anyone intent on retreating into the electronic world would have to go elsewhere. "People told me I'd tank," deCarrone said, "but business went up." That encouraged her to extend the ban to other electronic devices as well. "I hear a lot of people saying they wish more places would ban them; there's no energy. We all need our little parameters," deCarrone explained. "Telling people what your rules are is fair."

The value of a coffeehouse or other gathering place, deCarrone said, is that "people come and connect and they talk about politics. I think the city [government] gets nervous when people connect. The news—you've got it firsthand. It gives you ballast for your life. I hear people talking art and literature. My place promotes community, conversation, and connection."

The electronics ban sometimes leads to wry remarks. DeCarrone recalled the day when, she said, "everybody in the shop either had a book or was writing with a pen. One of them piped up and said, 'Oh, I forgot to ask you, should I be using a quill?'"

After twenty-four years of operating the shop, deCarrone decided in 2015 that it was time to do something else. She sold the business to an employee, David Oricchio, and a partner of his. Although they changed the name to East Rock Coffee and broadened the menu, they retained the prohibition on laptops, iPads, and tablets, both inside the shop and on the patio. Smartphones are allowed because, Oricchio said, "that's a more personal device than anything else." He said, though, that he has thought about

shelter." Hers was the first commercially sponsored outdoor gathering place in the neighborhood.

"Cities look cold," deCarrone observed. Outdoor seating "warms a city up," she said. "The very fact that people are out there brings out all the color of the people."

"letting people put the phones in a bucket while they're in the shop, and giving them a 10 percent discount."

"We get new customers every day, so we have to have the conversation with them" about electronic devices, he said. "We disappoint people all the time. But I think for the most part, people get it. A lot of people come in in pairs or single. They meet people here. We don't want people to disconnect from each other."

David Oricchio, behind the counter, retained a ban on laptops, tablets, and iPads when he acquired Lulu European Coffeehouse and changed its name to East Rock Coffee. Face-to-face conversation is key, he said. (Photo by Philip Langdon)

Orange Street Mobilizes

Late in the 1990s, a few neighborhood residents, including Kathleen
Wimer of the Ward 10 Democratic Ward Committee, architect Melanie Taylor, and a civic-minded landlord, Joseph Puleo, formed a group
called Upper Orange Street Neighbors. They were worried that some
of the businesses on Orange Street were not prosperous or stable. They
were also concerned that some blocks with multifamily houses east of
Orange Street were in danger of deteriorating as elderly owners moved
away or died.

Taylor drew up a statement of the group's mission: "to enhance the
quality of community life and further abundance in the lives of all people who live on and near Upper Orange Street" and "to support and
stabilize the community-based businesses along Orange Street." To
recruit members, "I put up posters in the neighborhood and invited
my neighbors to meet on my front porch," she said. All three East Rock
representatives on the board of aldermen attended an open discussion.

Yale University had by then launched the Yale Homebuyer Program,
which gave faculty and staff members incentives to buy homes in a few
beleaguered parts of the city; Yale subsidized the purchases over several years if the employees continued to own and live in them.[3] Upper
Orange Street Neighbors persuaded the university to extend the program to the not-so-steady blocks between Orange and State Streets. In
the years that followed, many Yale employees bought houses there, and
the rate of homeownership rose. Those blocks perked up.

Puleo built combination seating-planter boxes, which the group
placed at bus stops, and he installed bulletin boards at a few locations, including Lulu's, to let people know what was going on in the
neighborhood. The emerging New Urbanism movement, which pro-
moted walkable, mixed-use neighborhoods for people of varied ages,
incomes, occupations, and household composition, lent inspiration
to the Orange Street group. New Haven was where New Urbanism's

ideas about community had first germinated. Andres Duany, Elizabeth Plater-Zyberk, Robert Orr, Melanie Taylor, Patrick Pinnell, and other early leaders of the movement had studied at Yale and been influenced by Vincent Scully, an eminent professor of architectural history and urbanism.

As part of their class assignments, Scully's students often went to the top of East Rock and sketched the scene they saw spread out below. A spellbinding lecturer, Scully opened students' eyes to the logic, beauty, and social utility of traditional architecture, organized on a network of pedestrian-scale, tree-lined streets. New Urbanist ideas fit with Oldenburg's concept of the importance of gathering places. In East Rock and other neighborhoods that developed before modern separate-use zoning and before streetcars gave way to automobiles, there were stores and amenities within walking distance of most city-dwellers' homes, just as New Urbanism now prescribed.

Upper Orange Street Neighbors had a vision: creating inviting gathering places on the then-drab expanses of asphalt or concrete in front of several stores. Taylor believed that if perhaps three conspicuous and successful public spaces came into being, other merchants and building owners would catch the spirit and create more of them. Merchants could outfit these spaces with tables, chairs, shade umbrellas, and flowering plants, she said. The neighborhood group often referred to these public spaces as patios. DeCarrone, aware of the history of outdoor gathering places in Italy and elsewhere, called them plazas or piazzas.

The cost of developing patios scared some of the merchants and building owners, so the next question was, how could the expense be defrayed? The answer was to request aid from City Hall. Ultimately, the city was prevailed upon to extend its facade improvement program to the Orange Street corridor. The city made the program work by agreeing to a novel interpretation offered by Puleo: horizontal pavement would qualify as part of the facade.

It took several years for the idea to come to fruition, but from 2003 to 2007, matching grants of $20,000 to $30,000 apiece were disbursed for outdoor areas at Lulu's; at the Orange Food Mart and Orange Street Liquor Store, which shared a paved forecourt around the corner from the coffeehouse; and at Romeo & Giuseppe's, a high-quality grocer that had taken over an Orange Street space previously occupied by a lackluster Cumberland Farms convenience store.

In the overall scheme of things, the grants were not a lot of money—they were just enough to make the projects feasible—but the patios had the desired effect. Soon, people started to spend time at spots like Romeo & Giuseppe's sidewalk cafe. Matthew Feiner, an advocate of cycling, started having cyclists assemble at Lulu's on Saturday mornings and then head out on a 60-mile ride. The end point for their three-and-a-half hours of pedaling was Romeo & Giuseppe's, where they would eat lunch on the patio, two blocks from their starting point. The store did a large take-out business from a hot bar that prepared a variety of foods. "Romeo loves it," Feiner said of the postride gatherings. "In the summer, he'll come out and put down a pizza and say, 'Mangia.'"

Fun and Festive
Up and down the street, the atmosphere turned lively. A block north of Romeo & Giuseppe's, Caffe Bravo installed an outdoor seating area behind a low fence. When ownership of stores turned over, additional progress came. Joseph "Pino" Ciccone, who had been brought up in his family's food enterprises in suburban Branford, purchased the tired-looking Orange Food Mart. He kept on the experienced butcher, Jimmy Apuzzo, and changed the name of the store slightly, to P&M Orange Street Market, but otherwise transformed the place, updating its interior, introducing new products, and putting a larger emphasis on take-out dishes. Among those who used the market's patio were city firefighters, who at lunchtime parked their fire truck close by.

After a couple of changes of ownership, the Prime Market reopened as Nica's Market, also Italian. It was run by Giuseppe Sabino, who had been Romeo's hard-working, less voluble business partner until the two split up. At Nica's, Sabino installed a patio, too, a two-level affair acclaimed as the best one on the street, with the upper part of it shaded by a tall silver maple. Nica's did not win a facade grant. "Every time we applied, we were told there was no money," said Rosanna Sabino, Giuseppe's daughter.

As time went on, merchants no longer needed city grants to spiff up the appearance of their stores or build places where people would linger. Orange Street was prospering; the neighborhood's residents, and others from outside East Rock, found the patios irresistible. The combination—take-out food prepared on the premises and pleasant places to eat it—brought in substantial revenue. Customers stayed as long as they liked. The atmosphere was relaxed. The furnishings—movable chairs, metal tables, and shade umbrellas like those in Europe—were a hit with the public. Crime was no stranger to East Rock, yet the tables and chairs did not walk off, as pessimists feared.

In these outdoor spaces, there was less emphasis on rapid turnover than in indoor restaurants. I have never seen people being asked to leave because they had stayed at a table too long. Patio customers began arriving at 7:00 a.m., as soon as Nica's doors opened. At 7:30 p.m., when the market shut down for the night, people were still there, engaged in conversation. "It brings happiness to people," said Giuseppe Sabino.

Each place developed its own set of partisans. Police officers and firefighters flocked to P&M. Students from Wilbur Cross High School, a largely African American and Hispanic public school at the neighborhood's northern edge, used the patio and picnic tables in front of the One Stop Mart & Deli, a Syrian immigrant's shop selling Middle Eastern fare. Fans of Romeo & Cesare's, as Romeo & Giuseppe's was renamed after Giuseppe Sabino's departure, claimed that Nica's was more for "transients," short-term residents such as Yale graduate students. Bright-looking people in their twenties, some of them grad students, went in large numbers to Nica's, but whenever I stopped there, I also saw middle-aged and older people, including some who had been fixtures of the neighborhood for decades. The "transient" argument was wrong. There was a somewhat mixed and changeable group of people at nearly every patio on the street.

Some of the stores periodically organized parties with music, food, and drink. In September, a section of Orange Street was closed to vehicular traffic so that thousands of people, including artists, musicians, and entertainers, could participate in the annual East Rock Festival.

At P&M, Joel LaChance, a retired schoolteacher who years earlier had operated a bike shop downtown, brought a portable bike stand to a corner of the patio and started fixing flat tires and making other repairs. He is not charged for occupying the space; Pino Ciccone is happy to have him there. "Sometimes people want to sit near me just to watch and ask questions," LaChance said. "People are very interested in what I'm doing. I've made a lot of new friendships and acquaintances."

In 2009, Romeo joined two young partners, Bernard Massaro Jr. and Chris Mordecai, in opening yet another cafe on Orange Street. The new enterprise, Café Romeo, was an aesthetic departure, its styling sleek and contemporary. The cafe served breakfast, lunch, and dinner—from muffins and fresh fruit to soups, pizza from a wood-fired oven, and fig and goat cheese salads—for customers who carried their food and drinks to closely packed rows of metallic tables. On mild days, the cafe's glassy front panels slide out of the way, merging the interior and the patio into one continuous expanse. The cafe, including elaborate food preparation facilities, represented an investment, according to Romeo, of $800,000. Orange Street enterprises had become much more vigorous than they had been in the 1990s.

Today, New Haven savors its outdoor spaces. Chairs appear on some

Joel LaChance, with a portable bicycle repair stand that he pedals from his home nearby, works on bikes regularly on the plaza in front of the P&M Orange Street Market and the Orange Liquor Shop. (Photo by Philip Langdon)

patios by early March each year; people will sit at a table next to a mound of melting snow. On or close to Orange Street today are seven patios, all well used. The corridor has been energized.

Eva Geertz, a writer who lives on Orange Street, recalled that during one recent winter when a heavy snowfall made the street impassable to vehicles, "basically everyone in the neighborhood who could navigate the snow and was in good health went out to the streets, cups of hot chocolate in hand, to just . . . amble. It was like the entire length of Orange through East Rock became a huge, unofficial street party."

The tension between those inside a world-class private university and those on the outside is not likely to be eliminated by a series of gathering places. It should also be noted that these are not publicly owned spaces; people who want to hang out on a patio regularly are expected to buy something, even if it is just a cup of coffee. The important point, though, is that the atmosphere has significantly changed for the better, if not in all parts of East Rock, then certainly on Orange Street, a corridor that draws people from all across the neighborhood.

Will Baker discovered that although Whitney Avenue, carrying up to four lanes of fast traffic, has remained a corridor where pedestrians do not talk to one another on the sidewalk, Orange Street has become convivial. "They're only two or three blocks from each other, yet the sense of community and walkability is totally different," he said. "On Orange there's more of a sense of who's living around you. It's normal to have a conversation on the sidewalk with someone you know."

Seth Godfrey, who works at the New Haven public library, lives in a Whitney Avenue apartment and frequently goes to cafes on Orange Street. "To meet friends, it's the ideal place," he said. "You don't have

At Canner and Anderson Streets, a family established a Little Free Library in an old shipping trunk. They named it Goatville Free Library—Goatville was the historic name of one section of East Rock—and opened it for anyone who wanted to borrow or donate a book. (Photo by Philip Langdon)

to take a car. You don't have to waste valuable resources. I don't have a backyard. The cafe is the surrogate yard.

"It's just more social. You talk on a personal issue, on a film program at the library, local, international issues," Godfrey said. "Everybody needs a place to gather."

Taming Traffic

The City of New Haven has helped by making Orange Street safer for pedestrians and cyclists. Crews painted bike lanes—one lane northbound and one lane southbound—between the curbside parking and the travel lanes. Each bike lane is 4 feet wide, however, which Matthew Feiner, the local biking advocate, regards as less than ideal. Also, each bike lane is positioned close to parked cars, leading Feiner to call it the "door lane." The bike lanes have nevertheless made it clear that cyclists deserve a portion of the street.

The city painted stripes on many intersections to make crosswalks more visible. At some intersections, the city installed 4-foot-high plastic signs in the center of the pavement, warning drivers to slow down. In a city where motorists have a habit of racing through red lights, today drivers increasingly come to a halt when they see someone about to cross Orange Street.

Census figures show that to get to work, 36 percent of East Rock residents walk or bike, 14 percent use public transportation, and another 7 percent rely on a motorcycle, taxi, or carpool, not on driving alone.[4] More than twice as many East Rock residents ride a bike to work than did so in 2000.[5]

How Much Business Is Too Much?

Once businesses start to become popular beyond their immediate neighborhood, another question arises: Should limits be placed on their expansion? Having neighborhood businesses succeed is great, but

More Than a Block Watch

Periodically, there are bursts of crime—usually property crimes—in one part of East Rock or another. After a rash of car break-ins and apartment burglaries, approximately ten residents started the South of Humphrey organization, or SoHu, in 2007. The group focused on a small area below Humphrey Street and east of Orange Street.

"We decided we wanted to start a block watch," recalled Lisa Siedlarz, who, at midlife, lives in the second floor of the house she grew up in on Pearl Street, a narrow street of closely packed, predominantly one-, two-, and three-bedroom houses. Her brother Kevin lives on the third floor. An apartment on their ground floor brings in rental income.

Most block watches fade away once the emergency is over. SoHu is different. As the crime wave receded, SoHu evolved. "Two or three years into our existence, we realized that we were much more than a block watch," Siedlarz said. The group shifted to community-building. "We held a vote and decided to change our name from SoHu Block Watch to SoHu Neighborhood Association," she said.

"We did things to build community, so we would know who was living around us," she explained. For example, the group organized a program of "cookies and community" at a neighborhood church. "We started tree-planting," she said. "People would come, see what we were doing, and come next weekend. We planted 110 trees over the next four years. We only lost two. Each year we have a curb cleanup project. Last spring we planted perennials in the curb strips, weeded, mulched, and groomed trees."

if they become regional attractions, the volume of customers and traffic can undermine qualities that make the neighborhood an appealing place to live.

In East Rock, this issue has played out in a couple of ways. For decades, the section of the neighborhood from Whitney Avenue west to Prospect Street has had only one fairly insignificant cluster of shops, a line of storefronts facing Whitney Avenue. When a cheese shop downtown proposed opening a little beer-, wine-, and food-tasting business in one of those storefronts in 2010, a number of homeowners replied that they would love a gathering place of this sort. They had enjoyed

Today, SoHu counts more five hundred members on its four residential streets. Members stay informed through a listserv and through a variety of activities. "Along with tree planting and block parties, we also did two fund-raisers for the New Haven Police Department K-9 Unit, raising $10,000 in total. We posted notices about lost pets, and neighbors who needed assistance. We hosted movies in the park at College Woods [in East Rock Park], Halloween costume parades, and several other things," Siedlarz said.

"We have an annual block party every September because that's when new students move in. We welcome them," she said. "We now know our neighbors instead of being strangers. We look out for each other."

A block party in the center of Livingston Street on a September afternoon. (Photo by Philip Langdon)

the cafes on Orange Street and were eager to have a place to visit within walking distance of their homes. Several abutters of the proposed shop feared it might create a racket and opposed it. In the end, the proposal, which would have required a zoning variance, was withdrawn.

"I think there's a real tension between people who think it would be really nice to have a couple of places to walk to and those who think it would be the beginning of the end for the neighborhood," said William Kaplan, president of the Ronan-Edgehill Neighborhood Association, which represents homeowners west of Whitney Avenue. "Personally, I thought the limited wine-and-food business was a fine idea and would have been good for the neighborhood. But as president of the neighborhood association, I recognize that there are a variety of views on that subject, including the need to preserve zoning."

If zoning were widely breached, the quiet blocks in the western part of East Rock could lose their ambience, one offering relief from urban commotion. There is an argument for keeping commercial activity at arm's length, on Orange Street and State Streets, said Kaplan. "Walking to Romeo's [a half-mile or so from Ronan-Edgehill] is not an ordeal," he said.

On Orange Street itself, similar issues have arisen. For example, the owners of Nica's Market said that they desperately needed more parking, and in 2006, they built a parking lot for eighteen vehicles, set back slightly from the street. Neighborhood representatives, however, believed that Nica's had failed to make good on the market's promises to the community. So, three years later, when Nica's asked for a zoning variance to expand the store upward, including creating a dining area in the second story, neighborhood response was frosty, and the expansion proposal failed. People made it clear that they preferred shops geared mostly to the neighborhood, not businesses that grew much larger, attracted more car traffic, and generated more noise. Many residents believe that if a merchant wants to become a citywide or regional attraction, maybe the business should relocate to a larger, more commercial thoroughfare, such as State Street, which is only a couple of blocks away.

What has been helpful in neighborhood discussions is having a forum: the East Rock Community Management Team, which meets monthly to deal with neighborhood issues of all kinds. In the 1990s, the city established community management teams, made up of neighborhood residents, in every New Haven police district. "It's been a good clearinghouse for information," said Deborah Rossi, secretary of the East Rock team. "If you have a question about snow plowing, come to the meeting. If you have a question about crime, come to the meeting." Joe Puleo, a former leader of the team, said an informal rule gradually emerged:

developers who want to build something new or who want to convert an existing property to a different use present their proposals at the monthly meeting, which is public and generally runs for only an hour or a little more. The management team meetings—often attended by neighborhood alders and by the district police lieutenant—have become a way of guaranteeing that residents have a voice on potential changes.

When Oldenburg published *The Great Good Place* in 1989, he estimated that the United States had "probably lost half of the casual gathering places that existed at midcentury—places that hosted the easy and informal, yet socially binding, association that is the bedrock of community life."[6] In East Rock, the trend is in the opposite direction. The neighborhood has become progressively better supplied with places where people can meet, talk, express opinions, and learn. East Rock is a neighborhood where people walk and where, as time goes by, there are more and better places to walk to.

The Upper State Street Farmers Market was started by East Rock architect and developer Robert Frew and his wife, Susan, to bring reasonably priced vegetables and other foods to the neighborhood. (Photo by Philip Langdon)

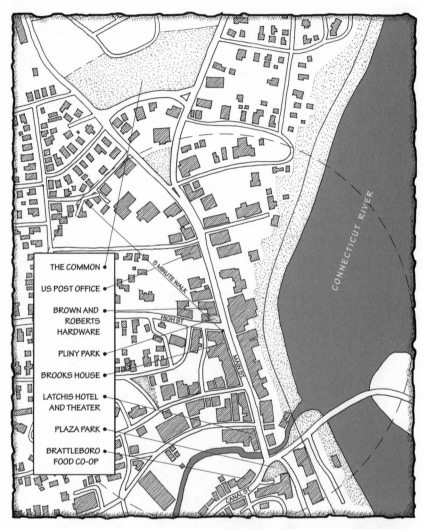

THE COMMON •
US POST OFFICE •
BROWN AND •
ROBERTS
HARDWARE
PLINY PARK •
BROOKS HOUSE •
LATCHIS HOTEL •
AND THEATER
PLAZA PARK •
BRATTLEBORO •
FOOD CO-OP

5 MINUTE WALK

HIGH ST

MAIN ST

CANAL ST

CONNECTICUT RIVER

Map of Main Street and nearby parts of Brattleboro, showing locations of important business and civic locations. (Drawing by Dhiru A. Thadani)

CHAPTER 3

Keeping the Town Center Vital: Brattleboro, Vermont

On trips in the 1990s to a cabin in the Vermont woods, I used to pass through Brattleboro, a town of 12,000 on the hilly west bank of the Connecticut River. What most impressed me about Brattleboro was its downtown. Main Street, the spine of the business district, looked busy and intact; it seemed as if this long-settled community, a dozen miles north of the Massachusetts line, had somehow been exempted from the decades-long withering away of American Main Streets.

Shops did business in the ground floors of the buildings, mostly red brick structures three or four stories high that had endured for more than a century. Offices and apartments occupied most of the upper floors; Brattleboro, heart of a trade area of about 35,000 residents, seemed not to have died from the top down, as many small-town business districts had been doing since the 1950s. On the sidewalks, there always seemed to be people going places. Brattleboro was largely rural, spread across 32 square miles of mostly hilly terrain, but more than 90 percent of its residents were clustered together at its eastern edge, no more than 2 miles from the well-preserved downtown.

As I drove north from the foot of Main Street, what first caught my attention was a four-story building in a buff color, a departure from the downtown's chiefly crimson complexion. It was the Latchis Theatre and Hotel, the only Art Deco structure in town. Within the multipurpose Latchis complex—hailed as "a town within a town all under one roof" when it opened in 1938—a visitor could order a meal, browse ground-floor shops, see a movie or a stage show, and get a room for the night.

Beyond the Latchis's neon-rimmed marquee, I noticed Sam's Army & Navy Department Store, a multilevel store that sold camping gear, canoes, athletic wear, casual clothing, and just about anything else a lover of the outdoors might want.[1] After that, I passed a coffeehouse, Mocha Joe's—shoehorned into a little space half above sidewalk level and half below it. In the blocks that followed, my eyes took in an old-style hardware store, a home furnishings retailer with the curious name "A Candle in the Night," a bank, and numerous other businesses.

After a fifth of a mile, the retail thinned out, and a parade of institutions began. On the west side of the street stood First Baptist Church, somber as a cemetery, with its tall Victorian Gothic tower and dark brick buttresses. On the east side stood the white-painted Centre Congregational Church, its elaborate wooden tower displaying the original town clock, made when James Madison was president. Before turning off Main Street toward Route 30 and the center of the state, I spotted a post office, the public library, and Brattleboro's municipal offices. The downtown seemed satisfyingly complete: all the core elements of town life were within a 10-minute walk. The distance from the foot of Main Street to the top was two-fifths of a mile.

Questions about Brattleboro percolated in my mind every time I drove through. How had this modest-sized town been able to keep its Main Street so vigorous? Brattleboro did not have a four-year college—the source of prosperity in many small towns—nor did it have a hoard of private wealth, yet it had kept its old buildings in good repair. It looked alive and energetic.

Brattleboro's Main Street, looking north toward the glass-roofed River Garden and Centre Congregational Church. The wooded hills to the right are across the Connecticut River in New Hampshire. (Photo courtesy of Stevens & Associates)

Curious to know more, I booked a room at the Latchis in 2007 and had a friend join me for a few days of exploring the area on bicycles. After some poking around, we realized that chain stores and national franchises were largely absent from Main Street. Decades earlier, the downtown contained national or regional retailers such as Montgomery Ward, F. W. Woolworth, and W. T. Grant, but those stores were gone. Newer chains had come, but mostly they clustered on automobile-dominated commercial strips like Putney Road to the north, not in the center of town.

The downtown had kept going, bolstered by a mix of Brattleboro natives and newcomers who, from the late 1960s on, had opened shops with imaginative personalities. Some, like Tom and Sally's Handmade Chocolates, founded by a couple who quit their financial careers in

Manhattan and moved to Vermont, won awards and lasted for years before fading from the local scene. Others became so embedded in community life that they continue to this day.

On Main Street and on tributaries like Elliot Street and High Street, the best retailers have been distinctive. Larry Simons, cofounder of A Candle in the Night, quotes a line from Nietzsche: "No true artist will tolerate, for one moment, the world as it is." Simons is an artist, a maker of assemblages from old, fallen-down wooden structures, as well as a man with a keen eye for indigenous handcrafts, which he has gathered on trips around the world and displayed in his import store.[2] A visitor from Denver stopped at A Candle in the Night and posted on Yelp: "Man, this is the most amazing furniture design store I've seen in years. They have stuff from India, Nepal, Africa, rugs from all over the world, and wonderful furniture."

A number of merchants and restaurateurs have put unusual spaces to use. The Hotel Pharmacy, named for where it started—in the Brooks House hotel on Main Street—occupied a decommissioned fire station for several years and then moved into a deconsecrated Methodist Church, where it remains. When I entered the store, sunshine streamed through high windows into a peak-roofed interior approximately 40 feet tall; it is the lightest, airiest drugstore I have ever experienced.

One evening, my friend and I went for dinner and drinks in the Mole's Eye, a pub in the semibasement of Brooks House. This French Second Empire building has presided since 1871 over the corner of Main and High Streets at the midpoint of downtown. Because the Mole's Eye was below ground, shielded from the sounds and activity outside, it felt like a refuge. Most Brattleboro enterprises do not retreat so insistently from the public eye—nor should they—but there is charm in finding the occasional recluse.

The belowground space I loved most was at Mocha Joe's, a coffeehouse in the scrunched-down base of a red brick building on the

Business is often brisk at the counter of Mocha Joe's Cafe, a coffeehouse that sits partly below sidewalk level. The cave-like atmosphere of the shop's main room makes it a place where people like to linger. (Photo courtesy of Mocha Joe's Roasting Company)

steepest section of Main Street. I found it awkward to enter the cafe, maneuvering down a set of recessed steps into a space that previously housed a shoe repair shop. Mocha Joe's offered no view of the street or the outdoors from its seating area, but the cave-like interior provided seclusion, which can be a welcome respite from a busy street. People do not want to be on public display all the time.

A 400-square-foot sanctuary of caffeine, coffee cake, conversation, and contemplation, Mocha Joe's is where a cross section of Brattleboro—and especially the town's artistic, lefty, countercultural elements—has been hanging out—sometimes gregariously and sometimes in communal solitude—since 1991. One Friday afternoon, a young man sat writing at a table across the room from me. He uttered not a word. The back of his black T-shirt said it all:

Drug free
Alcohol free
Tobacco free
Meat free
Dairy free
Egg free

At Mocha Joe's, a "free" man could share space with others who shared his outlook and some who did not. This being Brattleboro, the latter would be no doubt courteous about their differences.

A couple in a corner, beneath a shelf of books, played chess, gently laughing now and then. A young black woman (a small minority in Brattleboro, which is 94 percent non-Hispanic white) wrote on an iPad. A young man and young woman, about eighteen years old, sat close together on a black couch at the rear of the cave, working on a laptop. A woman about sixty years old and a woman half her age sat at another table, conversing, while a little girl accompanying them entertained herself with plastic blocks. Benjamin Zeman, a projects manager for the coffee roasting company, said of the cafe, "It's a community hub. The customers—it's everybody, all ages, all kinds of people."

Crucial to the functioning of Brattleboro is the town's compact, connected layout. People who live downtown or in the residential neighborhoods west of Main Street have ready access on foot or by bike to gathering places and to most essentials of daily life. Joelle Montagnino, in her late twenties, has lived in Brattleboro without a car for seven years; she walks and bikes everywhere. "I'm always seeing friendly faces," she said. "I lose count of how many times I say hello or smile at people downtown. Everyone is so interested in my future! There are plenty of spots downtown where I can hang out and read with a coffee."

The sidewalk of Main Street just down the slope from the entrance to Mocha Joe's Cafe is a favorite spot for young people to earn money selling art that they produced. (Photo by Philip Langdon)

A lot of young people live outside of town, where rents are cheaper, but they spend time in downtown Brattleboro because it is the liveliest spot in Windham County. They can catch "The Current," a Connecticut River Transit bus. "The bus drivers are personable and kind," said Zeman, "and they remember who you are."

The Roots of Brattleboro's Character

How did Brattleboro become a community that is physically and socially well connected? Geography exerted a crucial influence. In the early eighteenth century, the upper Connecticut River was on the frontier of British North America, which needed protection if English settlement was to expand. Fort Dummer—a blockhouse and stockade—was erected on the riverfront in 1724, and from its vicinity Brattleboro grew. Development expanded along streams such as Whetstone Brook, which raced down the hills to the Connecticut River. Water-powered mills produced lumber, furniture, paper, and woolens. In 1850, the railroad arrived, which encouraged industrialization. Printing became a local specialty, as did the manufacture of musical instruments.

The hills helped squeeze construction into a relatively small area, and the compactness of development magnified the town's liveliness. Lecturers often say that if you want to get an audience involved and active, put people in a room that is barely big enough to hold them. The same is true for communities.

Compressed development contributed to the town's physical charm. "The buildings are the right height," Dan Scully, an architect in nearby Keene, New Hampshire, said of Brattleboro's Main Street. At three to four stories, they are a full story higher than buildings on most Vermont Main Streets. They give the primary thoroughfare an unexpectedly robust, urban feeling. Robert Stevens, head of Stevens & Associates, a local engineering and architectural firm, described Main Street as a good "outdoor room," one in which "the buildings become walls; the walls

Stores, restaurants, and other businesses fill the ground floors of Main Street's three- and four-story buildings, while upstairs are apartments and offices. The height of the buildings creates a comparatively urban feeling. (Photo by Philip Langdon)

define the space." By his estimation, the proportions are right if the buildings are one to four times as tall as the street (including the sidewalk) is wide. In the commercial portion of Main Street, he observes, the buildings are approximately one-and-a-half times as high as the street is wide, so it feels right. The streets that enter downtown from the west—Flat Street, Elliot Street, and High Street—end in T intersections upon reaching Main Street rather than continuing through toward the river. T intersections are good for pedestrians and for safety in general. "You get a fraction of the accidents compared to a four-way intersection," Stevens pointed out.

In the 1960s, Interstate 91 was built a mile or so west of downtown. The new expressway did not siphon all the traffic away from the old

The grounds of the Brattleboro Retreat, north of the end of Main Street and the Brattleboro Common, are the site of the Green Expo that concludes the Strolling of the Heifers weekend. (Photo by Philip Langdon)

center. A steady stream of travelers from Massachusetts, Connecticut, and New York exited the interstate and drove down Canal Street and then up Main. As the first sizable town above Massachusetts' Pioneer Valley, Brattleboro has been able to continually introduce itself to skiers, hikers, vacationers, and others from the metropolitan areas to the south.

Another influence is the Brattleboro Retreat, founded in 1834 as the Vermont Asylum for the Insane. The Retreat maintains pleasant old buildings and grounds at the northern edge of downtown, where today it offers both inpatient and outpatient mental health and addiction treatment programs. The institution's staff brings to Brattleboro a cadre of well-compensated professionals who support Main Street enterprises and exert a liberalizing effect on the community. Never fenced off from the town, the Retreat, over the decades, has made area residents conscious of people with psychiatric troubles; patients have frequent outings, and townspeople often join the patients at events. Because of these interactions, the definition of community is more inclusive in Brattleboro than in many other towns.[3]

Windham County became a hotbed of the back-to-the-land movement of the late 1960s, probably because of its tolerance, inexpensive rural land, and accessible northeastern location, not to mention its cultural institutions, such as the Marlboro Music Festival, which each summer attracts thousands of people to the Marlboro College campus a dozen miles west of Brattleboro. Hippie communes, each with its own personality, cropped up in the countryside in the 1960s and 1970s. Farmers proved helpful to the young commune members, who arrived without much knowledge of how to grow things. Brattleboro newspaperman Norman Runnion summed up the local temperament this way: "Brattleboro tolerates as many different views as it has people with viewpoints, so long as no one gets pushy."[4] This open-mindedness has served the town well.

Taking the Initiative

When the center of town appears to be in jeopardy, local people go into action. Their responsiveness has been demonstrated repeatedly, as in the late 1990s, when Brattleboro had fifty-six empty storefronts, about thirty of them downtown. "We did some creative things to make the empty places look better—put art in them, make it look like something was going on," recounted Greg Worden, a former member of the Brattleboro Selectboard. Worden, a merchant who runs Vermont Artisan Designs, said the opening of a Walmart across the river in New Hampshire probably caused some of the store closings. Businesspeople worried that the town was in trouble.

Stanley "Pal" Borofsky, whose family has operated Sam's Army & Navy (now Sam's Outdoor Outfitters) since the 1930s, responded to the

The Strolling of the Heifers

In 2001, Dwight Miller, owner of a farm and orchard that his family had operated north of Brattleboro for seven generations, lamented to a neighbor: "Farmers are slowly going out of business. People don't know where their food comes from. If they knew how hard farming is, they'd support their local farmers."[a]

Fortunately, the woman he said that to was Orly Munzing, who had recently been to Pamplona, Spain, for the running of the bulls. From their conversation was born the idea of a Main Street parade that would promote the area's farmers and, in the process, bring crowds of people to downtown Brattleboro the first weekend of each June. Munzing and a group of volunteers, including downtown merchants, organized the Strolling of the Heifers. The first procession ambled up Main Street in 2002.

Future farmers from area schools and 4-H club members bring well-groomed heifer calves to town and walk them from the foot of Main Street to the town common, situated on a rise overlooking the Brattleboro Retreat. After the heifers come other farm animals—horses, mules, oxen, and sometimes goats, pigs, chickens, llamas, and alpacas—followed by tractors, clowns, floats, and bands.

The event has become a two-day affair that starts with a Friday evening street fair on Main Street that includes food, games, and music. The Saturday parade culminates in the Green Expo held on the grounds of the Brattleboro Retreat, featuring local food producers, regional craftspeople, cooking demonstrations, forestry and energy-conservation information, and shows by the Brattleboro-based New England Center for Circus Arts.

The stroll builds community spirit and introduces locals and visitors to

---

[a] Strolling of the Heifers, "Our Story," accessed Oct. 3, 2016, http://www.strolling oftheheifers.com/our-story/.

economic challenge by gathering several merchants, including Worden, and laying plans for an organization called Building a Better Brattleboro (BaBB). "People for years and years would do studies about what should be done," Worden recalled. "The plans would go on a shelf. Nothing would get done. We thought that one of the things that would help would be to have an organization to *do* some things."

restaurants, stores, artists, and other aspects of Brattleboro. Munzing, who has managed the stroll since it began, said some visitors first learn about it from media reports about the "Locavore Index," her organization's annual rating on how well each of the fifty states promotes locally sourced food.

As the parade and expo have become established, Strolling of the Heifers Inc. has also taken over operation of the River Garden. Activities there include an incubator for small businesses and a Farm-to-Plate Culinary Apprenticeship Program, which provides nutrition and culinary job skills to people on welfare, helping them find jobs in hospitality and food service.

Young cows, led mostly by boys and girls from towns around Brattleboro, head up Main Street in the annual Strolling of the Heifers. (Photo by Philip Langdon)

BaBB remedied some problems on its own. On issues that BaBB could not solve independently, it joined with the town government to find solutions. The town set up a downtown improvement district, supported by grants and by a special assessment on property owners. A facade improvement program upgraded the appearance of downtown buildings. A burnt-out former Rite-Aid pharmacy at one of the town's most visible locations, Main and High Streets, was razed, and on its site, BaBB constructed the Robert H. Gibson River Garden, a community building with a glass pitched roof and a rear deck offering a view of New England's longest river.

Across Main Street from the River Garden stood a vacant Dunkin' Donuts. BaBB (since renamed the Downtown Brattleboro Alliance) bought the building, demolished it, and installed a little park—Pliny Park—on the front portion of the land. The rear of the property was redeveloped as a Thai restaurant. So, in addition to having an attractive indoor gathering place at the River Garden, Brattleboro now has a small park where concerts are presented and where people can sit in comfort while waiting for a bus.

Increasingly, the town celebrated its artists and craftspeople and put their work on display. Since 1995, there has been a townwide Gallery Walk on the first Friday evening of each month; galleries and studios open their doors to the public, as does the Brattleboro Museum. Restaurants, cafes, and institutions complement those activities by exhibiting local art on their walls throughout the year.

The Battle of Hardware Stores

When Brattleboro's core businesses and services are threatened, townspeople act. In 2003, the world's largest hardware chain announced that it was going to open Home Depot store #4552 in a shopping center on Putney Road. The company chose a 60,000-square-foot space that had been vacated by a discount department store. Although it was just over half the size of the average Home Depot, people worried about the effect the store would have on local retailers, such as Brown & Roberts, a hardware emporium that the Putnam family had operated in the center of town since 1970. A citizens' group, BrattPower: Supporting Our Local Economy, organized a community forum and gathered 3,200 signatures on petitions opposing the Home Depot store. The group ran radio and newspaper ads outlining benefits of locally owned businesses and warning about the hidden costs of large chain stores.[5]

The Home Depot opened, but the community was prepared. Townspeople actually shopped more at Brown & Roberts than they had before. "There's a very strong local intention to keep money circulating in the area," said Wes Cutting, a building contractor who lives a few miles outside of Brattleboro. "I avoided patronizing Home Depot because I felt embarrassed by the possibility of running into one of my neighbors there. On one of my few visits to that store, I saw a business acquaintance and hid behind a display case rather than be seen shopping there."

"We had one of our best Christmas seasons ever," said Paul Putnam, one of the three Putnam brothers at Brown & Roberts. "Our customers were loyal. There was a lot of talk about supporting local hardware stores. People realized that if [existing local] stores went out of business, they wouldn't have a choice of where to shop."

The outcome was that the Home Depot closed its Brattleboro store in the spring of 2008 after four years of operation; it also closed fourteen stores in other locations that it judged to be generating too little revenue.[6] (Most Home Depot employees who lost their jobs were offered positions at the chain's stores in Keene, New Hampshire, or Greenfield, Massachusetts.) Residents were relieved that Brown & Roberts was still in business near the corner of Main and High Streets. Local loyalties had triumphed.

Fire at Brooks House

The gravest recent challenge to the viability of downtown Brattleboro was a fire that struck Brooks House, a mansard-roofed landmark of Main Street, on Sunday evening, April 17, 2011. Inside a wall, flames erupted where a metal staple had punched through an electrical cable years ago. The building's upper floors caught fire, and sixty-seven people had to be evacuated. The building that had been the centerpiece of Brattleboro since 1871—containing the Mole's Eye, Adagio's Restaurant, the Book Cellar, and other retailers, along with fifty-nine inexpensive apartments—was rendered uninhabitable.

In the following weeks, people organized impromptu festivals and other events, collecting more than $27,000 to help displaced residents. Governor Peter Shumlin came to town and told reporters that although the first thought was to bring in the wrecking ball, "engineers, the state, and the town of Brattleboro are working together to make sure we don't make any bad judgments."[7] The structure, which filled most of a block, remained largely sound, but extensive water damage meant that the interior would have to be gutted, fitted out, and brought up to current building codes. Repair would be an expensive proposition, difficult for a town that was not wealthy.

For months, the building sat empty. The Mole's Eye, the Book Cellar, and many of the other businesses never reopened. Murals were painted on plywood coverings to make the scene appear more hopeful. The building's owner, Jonathan Chase, wanted to revive the structure, which had long been in his family's hands, but after $1.5 million was spent stabilizing the structure, he concluded that the project was financially impossible and put the building up for sale. That precipitated a fervent hunt for local financial backers capable of bringing the project to completion. Mesabi LLC, a team of five investors led by engineer Robert Stevens, who had been involved in previous community efforts, stepped forward. It took the new group a long time to find a bank that would finance the project. Design and the search for funds consumed almost two years.

The renovation ultimately went forward with a price tag of $24 million, roughly three times what the 80,000-square-foot project was projected to be worth on the open market at completion.[8] Rents for business space were estimated to generate about $18 a square foot; Stevens pointed out that "$18 a square foot doesn't build anything these days." One thing that saved the building and reanimated the town's flagship corner was government programs, chief among them federal historic tax credits, New Market Tax Credits for low-income census tracts, and community development block grants. The dedication of local people was also crucial.

Some residents went as far as to deposit retirement savings into an individual retirement account that invested in Brooks House. Contributors were promised a 3 percent annual return for ten years. The investment was pitched as a "civic benefit," Stevens said, and residents stepped forward because "we needed every dollar we could get." He called this fund-raising technique "community-enabled development." This source of funding composed part of the project's $650,000 in community equity, which was essential to the project's reserves.

One lesson to be drawn from Brooks House is that a useful and attractive business district has staying power; people will work diligently to rescue it when it is in jeopardy. When a roadside commercial strip falls into decay, people mostly shrug their shoulders and drive on. They do not feel attached to big-box stores and drive-through restaurants. They do not sacrifice to save third-rate environments. A walkable downtown, on the other hand, is a place that people can identify with, and they will often work tenaciously to ensure its survival.

Brooks House reopened in August 2014. It was reconfigured to be one-third restaurant and retail space (on the ground floor and below), one-third office and college uses (on the first and second floors), and one-third residential, in the top floors. Two educational institutions—the Community College of Vermont and Vermont Technical College—moved into the building, bringing four hundred additional students downtown. Before they arrived, the number of college students downtown had been minimal. Marlboro College has operated a small Graduate and Professional Studies Center at the southern end

Brooks House after a community-led $24 million renovation. Duo restaurant anchors the corner of Main and High Streets. Two colleges, twenty-three apartments, and other commercial spaces are also in the building. (Photo courtesy of Stevens & Associates)

of downtown since 1997, and the School for International Training has run a graduate program in the countryside about 3 miles north of downtown. The two new state colleges considerably expanded Brattleboro's student population.

By 2016, all the office and residential space was occupied, and six of the eight retail units were leased, including the ground-floor corner, where a restaurant called Duo features ingredients grown within the region. Brooks House's top floors contain twenty-three apartments, ranging from a handful of rent-restricted units to market-rate two-bedroom units and a two-story penthouse. "This is the first time anyone has delivered high-end apartments downtown," Stevens pointed out. Retirees who have had homes in the countryside and who now want to live in the center of town, either part-time or full-time, rent many of them.

The next step is to turn a parking lot behind Brooks House into a public space, one that can host arts fairs, music, a farmers' market, and other events. A nonprofit organization has been set up to collect donations for this site, called Harmony Place. "The Downtown Alliance will partner to manage events in the space," Stevens said. "If you want an active public realm, someone has to manage it."

Making Pedestrians Comfortable

Like many New England towns, Brattleboro has streets and buildings that predate the automobile era. In many ways, this old-time layout works to the pedestrian's advantage. Commercial buildings come right up to the sidewalk, and some of them are narrow—about 40 to 60 feet wide—which gives people a constantly unfolding sequence of things to look at while they walk by. Many of the larger commercial buildings are divided at street level into narrow storefronts, which similarly adds visual interest for pedestrians.

The streets are extensively connected in the quirky New England way and intersect at varied angles. High Street flares out as it descends to meet Main Street, presenting a fine architectural panorama. Straight ahead is a jewel box of a building, three stories high and three bays wide, all dressed up with neoclassical accoutrements: fluted pilasters, lintels with keystones, and windows subdivided into small panes. Nearby are buildings with vigorously indented cornices or parapets, meeting the sky with strength and dignity. By capping the public space, those projections further define it.

Parking exerts a mixed effect on downtown and its walkability. On the one hand, some parking is essential as long as people travel in cars. In 2003, the town built its first (and only) public parking garage: a five-level structure accommodating three hundred vehicles. In its ground floor—testifying to the town's interest in more than one kind of mobility—is the Brattleboro Transportation Center, which coordinates transfers among regional and local buses and promotes Amtrak service and van pools. Surface parking is scattered through the downtown, mostly in small lots, some of them sitting behind the buildings they serve and thus detracting only minimally from the continuity of the streetscape. The town took the precaution of passing an ordinance prohibiting construction of new private parking lots, which could damage the streetscape.

On-street parking, on the other hand, is a feature that clearly benefits pedestrians. Much of Main Street is lined with on-street parallel parking. It gives motorists opportunities to park close to the stores, and it gives pedestrians on the relatively narrow 10-foot-wide sidewalks a sense of being shielded from moving vehicles, including heavy truck traffic.

Most residents regard Brattleboro as a good environment for walking. "It is very walkable and accessible," said Dylan Mackinnon, who moved to Brattleboro after growing up in Connecticut. "When you're walking along the streets outside of most [small community centers], motorists stare at you," he said, but not in Brattleboro. "Walking," he said, "seems to be part of the culture here."

"One thing the town has going for it is that from Brattleboro you can walk right out of town onto a variety of recreation trails," said George Weir, a consulting forester in nearby Newfane. "You can get out of town on foot and get some exercise." If you are ambitious, you can walk the bridge across the Connecticut River to New Hampshire, hike up Wantastiquet Mountain, and then walk back into downtown.

There is talk about further developing the town's walking and recreational network. The Vermont Downtown Action Team has called for creating an open-space network that would tie into the riverfront area and capitalize on features like Whetstone Brook. The brook would give people places to unwind, not far from the town's business and civic life.[9]

The town tries to ensure that people can get around on foot during the long winters. Using a snow plow about as wide as a golf cart, the

The Town of Brattleboro extended the sidewalk into Main Street at its intersection with Elliot Street to make conditions safer and more comfortable for pedestrians. (Photo courtesy of Hannah O'Connell, Town of Brattleboro)

public works department clears approximately 14 miles of sidewalks, mostly at the edge of downtown and on routes where children walk to school. In the downtown itself, the building and store owners are responsible for keeping their sidewalks clear.

People were alarmed when three pedestrians in Brattleboro were killed by motor vehicles in 2012. A community group, the Brattleboro Safe Streets Project, has advocated safety improvements, and the town government has been responding.[10] The town established midblock crossings on some long blocks and has been devising ways to make the crossings more noticeable to oncoming vehicles. "One recent initiative that is working very well at midblock crosswalks is the installation of flashing lights that activate only when a pedestrian pushes a button," Town Manager Peter Elwell said. Experience shows that if a signal flashes all the time, 40 percent of drivers will stop, Elwell said, but if it flashes only when someone pushes the button, vehicles will halt 85 to 90 percent of the time.

Downtown sidewalks have been extended into the street at some corners in an effort to coax drivers to slow down and to reduce the distance that pedestrians have to cross. As an added benefit, these safer sidewalks promote sociability. "Where the sidewalk becomes wider, people tend to gather," especially during events like parades, Elwell said. "There's public take-back of that space." Besides making physical improvements, the town has recognized the need for a conscious, clearly understood structure for making decisions on safety matters. Thus, Elwell said, "the public knows how we approach this, and they know how to address the town government with ideas or proposals."

The Importance of Reciprocity

Downtown Brattleboro retailers struggle against serious economic limitations. As of 2014, household income in Brattleboro averaged about $41,000 compared to $53,000 for Vermont as a whole and just under $53,000 for the United States.[11] Employment has been buffeted by bank consolidation, closing of the Vermont Yankee nuclear power plant on the Connecticut River, and the move of two sizable companies to locations outside of downtown. Taxes are higher and more numerous in Vermont, with its communitarian ethic, than in "live free or die" New Hampshire. Although there are rarely many vacancies, turnover in downtown retail buildings is substantial. Big-box stores on the New Hampshire side of the river have cut into Brattleboro's retail trade. Brattleboro is a dining, cultural, and entertainment destination, though, and vacationers and owners of second homes in the mountains like going to the local stores, galleries, and restaurants. The sidewalks on Main Street are busy with locals on weekdays and with lots of out-of-towners on weekends.

Distant visitors return again and again to stores like Sam's, known for outdoor wear and casual clothing with reasonable prices. "You build a relationship with the customers," said Pal Barofsky, whose family started Sam's in the 1930s and still runs it. "They remember the store and they come back." Brattleboro's retail successes reflect a basic axiom: people tend to be loyal to local businesses that treat them considerately.

Little courtesies abound. While watching youngsters lead animals up Main Street during the Strolling of the Heifers, I noticed a line of parade-goers waiting to use the restroom at Mocha Joe's, and nobody was required to make a purchase there. When I asked Benjamin Zeman of Mocha Joe's about it, he said that there has never been a "customers only" policy, on stroll day or any other. "I think a lot of Brattleboro is like that," he said. "We are a very hospitable little town."

Paul Putnam at Brown & Roberts told me something similar about the small parking lot behind the hardware store. He has often seen cars parked there when their owners were not shopping in the store. Putnam's attitude is to let them park, a policy that fosters goodwill. Said Putnam, "They're our customers. They're just not our customers at the moment." Putnam believes that Brown & Roberts, which his father and a partner purchased in 1970, has endured by listening to customers' desires. "If we got two or three requests for something, we thought maybe we should be carrying it," he said. "The first few years, we kept adding inventory and adding inventory so that we'd have what the customer wants. It didn't matter whether the customer spent seventy-nine cents or seventy-nine dollars. The key was to have what the customer wants. We earned their loyalty. On average, we probably had 50 percent more merchandise per square foot than the average hardware store."

In 2013, when Putnam turned sixty-five, Paul and his brothers sold Brown & Roberts to the owner of five other Vermont hardware stores. The new owner reduced the inventory a bit, yet the overall philosophy did not change, said Putnam. He continues to work part-time in the multilevel store, where creaking wooden floors with humps and valleys announce a person's movements. "We've always been very fair with our

Keeping the Co-op Downtown

A key element of a walkable community is a conveniently located grocery store. In downtown Brattleboro, the Brattleboro Food Co-op fills that role.

The co-op got its start in 1975 in the garage, and later in the dirt-floored basement, of the Green Mountain Health Center. Initially a buying club for a small number of households, it evolved into a 2,000-square-foot storefront space and then, in 1988, into an 11,000-square-foot store in Brookside Plaza, a small shopping center near the foot of Main Street. By 2002, with about six thousand active shareholding members plus many other customers who did not own shares, the co-op felt the need to expand again. The question was, would it leave downtown?

"A developer approached us," said Alex Gyori, the store's longtime general manager, now retired. "He asked us, 'Would you consider moving out?'" The idea was to put the co-op into a 45,000-square-foot former supermarket space in a shopping center on Putney Road, north of downtown. The location offered "all the parking you could dream of," Gyori said. In large committee meetings and in small group sessions, the co-op wrestled with the pros and cons. "People didn't talk about food," Gyori recalled. "They talked about the co-op's role in the community."

The civic organization Building a Better Brattleboro thought the co-op should stay downtown, where it would serve as a community anchor, much like Sam's Outdoor Outfitters, the Latchis complex, and the Brown & Roberts hardware store. In 2004, the stay-downtown position triumphed, and the co-op bought the nearly four-acre Brookside Plaza. In 2009, the co-op decided to raze the plaza and erect a new 15,000-square-foot store in that central location, where Main Street meets Canal Street.

The store would occupy the ground floor, and the co-op's offices and a demonstration kitchen where people could learn about nutrition and healthy eating would occupy the second story. That might have been the end of the decision making, but as Gyori noted, "a number of people in town were concerned with affordable housing. Many of them were co-op members." Ultimately, the co-op decided to add housing to the project by teaming up with the nonprofit Windham & Windsor Housing Trust. A financially complex arrangement was devised under which the trust paid to add two stories to the building. Managed by the trust, these top two upper floors today contain twenty-four apartments, with three levels of affordability so that people of modest income can live there.

Connie Snow, executive director of the Windham and Windsor

Housing Trust, points out that placing apartments above the grocery store and its offices produced a four-story building, which makes a more urban streetscape. Waste heat from the store's refrigeration equipment is recycled to heat the apartments. Clad mostly in Vermont slate, the co-op building, designed by Gossens Bachman Architects and completed in 2012, has strengthened Main and Canal Streets. "The downtown needed support," Gyori said. "It needed a business that would attract people downtown." Indeed, it got one.

That is a familiar Brattleboro theme: people speak up for keeping essential activities in the center of town where everyone, including those who do not drive, can reach them. Brattleboro has people who see themselves as neighbors and citizens, not simply as consumers or business operators.

The Brattleboro Food Co-op's new store and offices, which opened in 2012, fill the bottom two stories of this building at Canal and Main Streets. The upper floors contain affordable apartments. (Copyright by Peter Mauss/Esto, courtesy of Gossens Bachman Architects)

prices. People want to shop here because they know we're fair," he said.

This attitude holds true across a range of enterprises. Matthew Blau, a chef who has opened a series of restaurants in Brattleboro, started at the top of the price spectrum. "Fifteen years ago, I was only feeding people who could spend $100 a meal," he said. "Now I'm feeding people who want to spend $20. I keep going steadily down in price points." He's done that because of many residents' limited incomes, but also because his outlook has shifted. "People need to have a good hot, filling meal for twelve bucks or less," he said. "Have it be wholesome, have it be quick." In 2014, he opened Milagros Mexican Kitchen, a Main Street eatery where an overstuffed bean and cheese burrito with Mexican rice, lettuce, and fresh salsa cost $5.95. Customers picked up their meals at a counter and carried them to their tables, eliminating tipping.

The food was good when I tried it, but the economics did not work in a county where, as of 2013, 12.4 percent of households lived in poverty. Milagros lasted only into 2015 before shutting down. Blau is persistent, though: he switched to another economy-minded concept and opened a new restaurant, Brattleburger, in the same location.[12]

In a town of Brattleboro's size, he said, "You need a slice of every demographic." He believes that every group can be served on Main Street. "It's very important that we're right downtown," he emphasized. "Each year, we get more people living close in. I think a lot more people ride their bikes in. And people are just walking more. Walking distance to downtown used to be two blocks; now it's three-quarters of a mile."

A Changing Community

"Downtowns are never stagnant," said Donna Simons, co-owner of A Candle in the Night. "The job of trying to maintain the vitality and vibrancy of downtowns is very hard work, and it's always changing."

Brattleboro pays increasing attention to what people do with their leisure time. "The trend now in downtowns that are somewhat alive is to become cultural and entertainment centers, with some stores," said Simons. "That's really the model." Restaurants, cafes, and art galleries fit that concept perfectly, but everyday functions matter, too. One reason downtown Brattleboro is appealing is that it still serves many everyday needs. These functions—shopping for groceries, buying clothing, dropping into hardware stores and pharmacies, visiting the library and the post office, going to the town offices, and maybe going to church—underline Brattleboro's genuineness. Brattleboro works for everyone.

In the future, the community would benefit from having more people living downtown. An expanded population—especially if the residents are neither all low-income nor all affluent—would further animate the center of town and keep a varied business life afloat. Certain kinds of retail might be added. Specialty food stores, complementing the Brattleboro Food Co-op, could do well. Consultants have identified opportunities for specialty retail—especially clothing—and for personal care stores such as bath, cosmetics, and day spas.[13] Upscale enterprises would be fine as long as they do not squeeze out the necessities.

People need to be engaged in their community, and engagement depends on frequent human contact and conversation. As Scot Mackinnon, father of Dylan Mackinnon, said, "From a political perspective, walkable towns are easier to govern because the citizens still make regular eye contact with one another." Scot Mackinnon, who operates a farm in East Haddam, Connecticut, southeast of Hartford, and who has served as a selectman in that town, continued, "It typically takes much less energy for elected officials to suss out support for an initiative in a walkable community than it does in an automobile suburb. In my beloved East Haddam, an auto suburb with two underused commercial villages, there is less walkability, and therefore support for a given policy can be very unpredictable. If politicians do not have informal, quotidian ways to interact with their constituents, they are missing a vital tool of governance."

The Celebration Brass Band plays on Main Street near Elliot Street during the Friday evening street festival that leads up to the Strolling of the Heifers on the first Saturday each June. (Photo by Philip Langdon)

Wes Cutting, the building contractor, offers another view on the reasons Brattleboro functions as well as it does. He sees many of Brattleboro's offerings, particularly its art galleries, craft shops, and bookstores, as springing from the "real interest in the town in literature, music, and the arts." He said, "It just feels wonderful to go into those shops. I think, a lot, it's really the spirit of the people, wanting to do it."

Cutting added, "I think underlying Brattleboro's vital feeling is people's desire to be here and living this way. It has more to do with a felt connection with the area and with each other. Under that is a quest to discover and live what is of true value in this life. I think there is a commitment to value connection over commerce. The dialogue between those two positions is a dynamic one in this community—maybe in other walkable communities also."

Parker Huber, who lives along the river not far north of downtown, came to Brattleboro in 1983, attracted by its character and its social activities. He was in a folk-dancing group at the time and appreciated Brattleboro's enthusiasm for the arts. "It's my theory that artists have the sensitivity to the place and can be creative," he said. Huber gets around town on a bike and sees the community's scale as crucial. "Its smallness is something I feel is vital to it," he said. "If you get too much, it takes that spirit away."

Richard Wizansky, who in 1968 was one of the founders of the county's most famous commune, Packer Corners Farm, is now a consultant with a doctorate in education. He still lives in the area. To him, the appeal of Brattleboro is rooted in friendliness and familiarity. "Part of the pleasure of walking in Brattleboro is meeting so many people that you know," he said. "It's a talkfest. That makes walking down Main Street fun. It makes you feel you're walking in 'My Town.'"

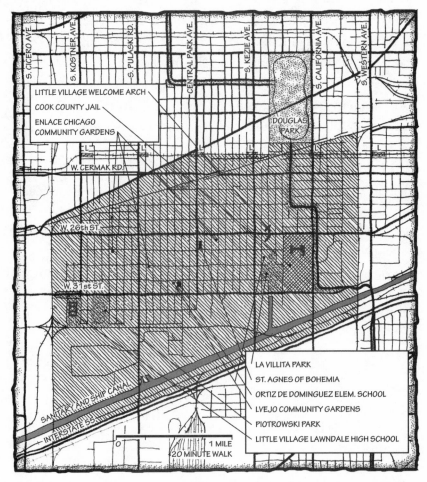

Little Village is shaded in this map, which shows part of the Southwest Side of
Chicago. The community is laid out in a grid of east–west and north–south
streets. On Little Village's edges are large tracts of land that used to contain
industries. (Drawing by Ben Northrup)

CHAPTER 4

The Walkable Immigrant Neighborhood: Chicago's "Little Village"

City neighborhoods often take on new identities as one population moves out and another moves in. Little Village, on the Southwest Side of Chicago, has gone through changes of name and population more than once.

If you had boarded a train in downtown around 1880 and ridden it 5 miles southwest, you would have arrived not in a place called Little Village but in a subdivision called Lawndale. The founders of Lawndale, real estate developers Alden C. Millard and Edwin J. Decker, started converting farmland on the city's outskirts into lots for houses, stores, churches, and meeting places shortly before the great Chicago fire of 1871.[1] Their expectation was that Lawndale, an orderly new community just a 20-minute ride from downtown, would appeal to businesspeople, professionals, and other middle-class Chicagoans.

In fact, affluent families, including meatpacker E. G. Orvis, did come and erect a number of stately houses, some of them architect-designed. By the 1890s, however, manufacturing and other industry also descended on the Southwest Side, bringing with them tens of thousands of blue-collar workers, many of them immigrants. The Anglo-Saxon upper middle class shifted to less ethnic pastures.

Lawndale and an adjacent area known as Crawford became home to thousands of Bohemians, immigrants or children of immigrants who had roots in what is now the Czech Republic. They found Lawndale agreeable in that it was tidier and less crowded than Pilsen, the neighborhood immediately to the east, where many Czechs had endured the difficulties of tenement life. In Lawndale, they established a host of Czech-oriented institutions, including, in 1904, Blessed Agnes of Bohemia Roman Catholic Church (now St. Agnes of Bohemia), the neighborhood's largest Catholic parish. By World War I, so many Bohemians had settled in Lawndale that they began calling it Czech California.

As time went by, the southern portion of Lawndale became known as South Lawndale, distinguishing it from its near twin, North Lawndale, a Czech stronghold that changed composition during the 1920s and emerged as Chicago's most populous Jewish settlement. South Lawndale remained a stable working- and middle-class community into the 1950s. It was an area where Czechs owned most of the stores and where smaller contingents of Poles, Germans, Hungarians, and other Europeans lived side by side with the Czechs.

Then came a period of rapid racial change, reflecting the migration of hundreds of thousands of southern blacks to Chicago in the 1940s, 1950s, and 1960s. African Americans, long confined to what was referred to as the Black Belt on the city's South Side, surged into neighborhoods that had previously used deed restrictions and other means to keep them out. North Lawndale underwent the most abrupt racial turnover in the entire city; at the start of the 1950s, it was 87 percent white, and at the end of that decade, it was 91 percent black. Many African Americans could not buy houses except at inflated prices, through exploitative contracts rather than standard mortgages. North

Lawndale started to fall apart. In 1964, business leaders in South Lawndale responded by rechristening South Lawndale "Little Village," a name meant to clearly distinguish the white ethnic community from its collapsing black neighbor.

As conceived by Czech American real estate salesman Richard Dolejs, the name Little Village was supposed to suggest a picturesque European village—there were plans, not widely implemented, to decorate the storefronts in a quaint, Central European style—but the 1960s held a further surprise. A huge wave of immigrants was ready to move west from Pilsen, and that group was Mexican—not European—in origin. By 1980, the majority of Little Villagers were Mexicans or descendants of Mexicans. Some held US citizenship. Many did not.

At that point, the neighborhood might have tumbled into disrepair given that the Mexicans who had moved there generally had low incomes and not much schooling; many were not fluent in English. To make matters worse, in the mid-1960s, Latino gangs began operating in Little Village. (They remain active to this day.) The neighborhood persevered nonetheless. Mexican migrants diligently sought work at whatever level they could find. They squeezed their families into small apartments, often sharing the homes of relatives at the start. Their numbers grew phenomenally. From 1960 to 2000, Little Village's population soared 50 percent, from slightly less than 61,000 to slightly more than 91,000. Now, there were more customers than ever for the neighborhood stores, more people to stroll the sidewalks, and more participants (at least potentially) for efforts aimed at improving the neighborhood and boosting the prospects of its people. If South Lawndale had been "Czech California" from the 1920s to the 1950s, Little Village proudly presented itself as the "Capital of the Mexican Midwest" from the 1970s onward. It became the principal port of entry for people migrating from south of the Rio Grande to the north-central United States.

Mural on a garage. Much of the public painting in Little Village echoes Mexican motifs. (Photo by Philip Langdon)

Coping with Calamities

I first learned of Little Village from Eric Klinenberg's book *Heat Wave*. Klinenberg, a sociologist, investigated the effects of a catastrophic heat wave that struck Chicago in July 1995. The heat index, a combined measure of temperature and humidity, soared to more than 100 degrees Fahrenheit and stayed there for an entire week. On two straight days, it exceeded 115 degrees.[2] The extreme conditions caused the deaths of 739 people across the city. Most victims were elderly and lived alone, expiring in isolation in their sweltering apartments. A death toll of this magnitude had never been seen before in a heat wave in the United States.

In probing the disaster, Klinenberg discovered interesting patterns. The death rate, he noticed, varied greatly from one neighborhood to another. One of the starkest contrasts was between North Lawndale and Little Village. North Lawndale suffered a horrific death rate—40 fatalities per 100,000 residents—whereas Little Village had fewer than 4 deaths per 100,000. North Lawndale and Little Village had similar microclimates and had "almost identical numbers and proportions of seniors living alone and seniors living in poverty," according to Klinenberg, yet from the standpoint of public health, Little Village was a different world, ten times safer than its neighbor.[3]

Why was there this disparity? Some believed that Little Village came through the heat wave better than North Lawndale because Latinos maintain strong family ties across the generations—ties that are crucial during a crisis—and Latino family connections saved the neighborhood's elderly. Klinenberg cast doubt on that explanation. For one thing, nearly half the elderly in Little Village at the time were not Latino; they were white non-Hispanics (most likely Czech Americans or Polish Americans) who had stayed behind when their compatriots had moved to suburbs like Cicero and Berwyn.

Instead, Klinenberg hypothesized that something in Little Village's social environment enabled vulnerable people to survive a period of intense physical stress. The keys, he deduced, were the neighborhood's "busy streets, heavy commercial activity, residential concentration, and relatively low crime."[4] Those factors, he observed, "promote social contact, collective life, and public engagement in general and provide particular benefits for the elderly, who are more likely to leave home when they are drawn out by nearby amenities." In Klinenberg's view, it is critically important that vulnerable people, such as elderly individuals who live alone, have access to "comfortable and secure streets and sidewalks" and to places that "draw people out of their homes and into the public." When those are readily available, people establish relationships; they learn where to turn during an emergency.

North Lawndale, a largely African American neighborhood, contained few stores and gathering places within walking distance of homes, and crime shadowed the streets. In Little Village, the opposite was true. Elaborating on ideas from Jane Jacobs, Klinenberg asserted that "a substantial quantity of stores and other public places sprinkled along the sidewalks of a district is the basic requisite for establishing public safety through informal social control. Commercial institutions draw residents and passersby out into the sidewalks and streets, inviting foot traffic and promoting social interaction among consumers, merchants, and people who simply enjoy participating in or observing public life."[5]

Twenty-Sixth Street

"Bienvenidos a Little Village," says the greeting on a decorative arch that stretches across Twenty-Sixth Street near the corner of Albany Avenue. This ceremonial spot, a short distance west of the massive, grim Cook County Jail, is where costumed dancers, riders on horseback, motorcyclists wearing oversized sombreros, and young women clutching red, white, and green flags assemble in mid-September each year for the Midwest's largest Latino parade. Two hundred thousand people—some of them residents of Little Village, others from as far away as Iowa and Michigan—line the street for twenty-five blocks, celebrating Mexico's Independence Day.

Twenty-Sixth Street, the chief commercial corridor in Little Village for more than a century, is a good route for the parade. It is a corridor amply endowed with Mexican-oriented products, stores, and ambitions. During the noisy 2-mile procession, the parade's participants pass street vendors peddling *aguas frescas*, a sweet drink of fruits, cereals, flowers, or seeds blended with sugar and water. They pass *panaderias*, bakeries selling *pan dulce* (sweet bread), *bolillos* (variants on the French baguette), *cuernos* (horn-shaped pastries), and other Mexican treats. Eight of these aromatic establishments operate within Little Village's 4.4 square miles.

They pass eighty restaurants, including Mexican ones like Nuevo Leon, where customers order northern Mexican dishes such as *machaca*,

View toward the arch on West Twenty-Sixth Street. One of the men in the sketch points to where Little Village is situated in the city of Chicago. (Drawing by Dhiru A. Thadani)

rehydrated dried meat pounded into tenderness and served with large flour tortillas. They pass shops selling bridal gowns and *quinceañera* dresses, frilly, floor-length outfits that Mexican American girls wear to their fifteenth-birthday parties. There are thirty-eight *quinceañera* dress shops on Twenty-Sixth Street.

In all, more than a thousand businesses line the 2-mile-long commercial corridor. Toward the end of the Czech period, Little Village had seen an increase in the number of vacant stores. The 26th Street Community Council and the Twenty-sixth Street Chamber of Commerce (now the Little Village Chamber of Commerce) set about recruiting businesses to fill them. Owners of neglected buildings were prodded to fix them up. Within a few years, the empty storefronts were occupied and active again. Today, besides shops with a Mexican flavor, there are hundreds of

A vendor selling snacks from a food cart on West Twenty-Sixth Street in Little Village. The bags hanging from the cart's ceiling contain imitation chicharrones, a Latino treat. Real chicharrones are deep-fried pork skins; imitations are made from flour and water. (Photo by Philip Langdon)

mainstream enterprises: banks, discount stores, dry cleaners, insurance agencies, grocery stores, doctors' offices, beauty salons, check-cashing and money-transfer outlets, shoe stores, and dollar stores. Listen to local people and you will repeatedly hear that Twenty-Sixth Street in Little Village has a greater sales volume than any other business district in Chicago except posh North Michigan Avenue. Its robust performance is a point of pride.

Stores within Walking Distance

The standard Chicago grid of streets and alleys is a structure that helps make neighborhood businesses accessible. From any side street in Little

Las Isabeles, a corner grocery at South Central Park Avenue and West Twenty-Seventh Street, where a vendor displays fruits and vegetables for sale. The mural offers a religious message: "As I have loved you, you also should love one another." (Photo by Philip Langdon)

Village, residents can walk directly to Twenty-Sixth Street. There are no dead ends or cul-de-sacs to interfere with access. Twenty-Sixth Street, 48 feet wide from curb to curb, provides two lanes down its center for the 14,000 vehicles that travel it each day, plus two lanes providing on-street parking. There are 10-foot-wide sidewalks between the street and the storefronts, a width not overly generous but sufficient. The sidewalks get heavy pedestrian use, especially on weekends.

Commerce is also concentrated along a few other streets, and sprinkled throughout the neighborhood are corner stores. When the Czech owners moved out, many of the corner stores they had operated were bought or leased by Mexican residents, who have now run them for two or three generations. Neighbors close by, especially last-minute shoppers, stop in them frequently for milk, juice, and popular Mexican items such as *menudo* (tripe soup) and *carnitas* (deep-fried pork). "There's a corner store on just about every block," said Simone Alexander, a community organizer with Enlace Chicago, a dynamic community development organization serving Little Village. "People walk to the bank and they walk to the grocery store. A lot of women walk their kids to doctors' appointments."

Since 2000, Little Village's population has slipped to 79,000, largely because Mexico-US migration has gone into reverse since the world economic crisis of 2008. The Chicago area still has the second-largest population of Mexican-born immigrants in the United States, but Illinois has lost hundreds of thousands of construction, manufacturing, and other industrial jobs in recent years, work that used to lure Mexicans northward.[6]

Little Village nevertheless remains densely populated, at nearly 18,000 persons per square mile, with higher concentrations in some areas. Although the median household income in Little Village is $34,000 a year—far below the national average of $52,000 and the metro Chicago average of $71,000—the volume of households per square mile generates enough spending to keep plenty of businesses afloat.

How many households might be within a 1- to 4-minute walk of a corner store? The standard house lot in Little Village is 25 feet by 125 feet, and a block generally contains about fifty lots. So, a single block could hold 50 bungalows, or 100 apartments if it is developed with two-family units, or 150 apartments if it is filled with three-family units. In an area uniformly developed with three-family units—which are common in the eastern portion of Little Village—there could be more than nine hundred households within a 4-minute walk of the store. Many buildings in Little Village have been reconfigured to add more apartments than zoning allows, so the customer base of some

Mural of Our Lady of Guadalupe on the side of La Chiquita Supermercado on South Pulaski Road. The brightly colored center of the mural, one of the older ones in Little Village, is based on a painting in the Basilica of Our Lady of Guadalupe in Mexico City. (Photo by Philip Langdon)

corner stores may be even greater than these calculations indicate. (The median household in Little Village contains 3.8 occupants, nearly triple the density of Chicago as a whole.)

Corner stores are only the beginning. A variety of other small businesses operate in houses, garages, and backyards. Many jobs filled by Mexicans do not pay well, so a man with mechanical skills may set up an auto repair shop part-time in his garage to bring in extra income. "We've got loads of alley mechanics," said Andrea O'Malley Muñoz, a Little Village resident since the 1970s. The mechanics live close to their customers, charge reasonable prices, and speak Spanish, all of which builds a following, Muñoz said. "Some of them do quite well," she noted. Those who prosper may eventually move their operation to a larger garage, on a street with more visibility.

Sprinkled through the neighborhood are fabricators of the metal fences that enclose most of Little Village's front yards. Also scattered through the neighborhood are tire shops. "You drive through, and you're back out on a main street," Muñoz said. "It's faster than the AAA."

People who live in Little Village tend to spend money in Little Village. Although car-owning residents shop some of the time at big-box stores in nearby Cicero, loyalty to community businesses is pronounced. "Little Village functions because people sort of stay in the community," Matt Cole of Chicago Neighborhood Housing Services observed. "They say, 'This is my community, this is where I shop.'" For residents who need products and services, "there's not a lot of reason to leave," said community organizer Alexander. "You can get what you want in Little Village—unless you're in your twenties or thirties and looking for craft beers."

Peddling for a Living

There are many ways in which a dense, gridded neighborhood like Little Village helps some of the new residents to earn a living. It might not be a generous living, but enough to get by on. The most conspicuous example is street vending. With a minimal outlay, a new person from Mexico can rent or buy a pushcart, stock it with a few simple foods, and start peddling. Vendors find good locations on major streets, street corners, and even side streets. Their presence makes the streets safer and more sociable. "It adds to the vibrancy of the streets," said Ricardo Muñoz, who has represented Little Village on the Board of Aldermen since 1993. "It's another set of eyes and ears."

Andrea Muñoz (unrelated to the alderman) described the daily rhythm of the peddlers: "In the morning there are three or four different groups of vendors. The earliest are those selling tamales and warm drinks. They are out from 6 to 10 a.m., catching people on the way to work, serving a mobile breakfast." Tamales are accompanied in cold weather by *atole*, a flavored, corn-based drink similar to hot chocolate.

Other peddlers arrive to sell *churros*, crunchy fried-dough pastries, sometimes sprinkled with sugar, that serve as a quick breakfast or snack. They are good for dipping in *champurrado* (chocolate-based atole) or *cafe con leche* (strong coffee mixed with scalded milk).

Around 10 o'clock, the tamale vendors depart, and another group of peddlers—the *eleteros*—appears. This group sells fruit (watermelon, cantaloupe, honeydew melon), corn, cucumber spears, bags of artificial pigskin, and *raspas* (flavored ice shavings). The fruit is cut or chopped and sprinkled with lime juice, often with a dash of red pepper for kick. Corn (*elote*) is this group's biggest seller, which is why these peddlers are called eleteros. The corn is served on a stick or as kernels in a cup. A healthy lunch or snack from an eletero costs the customer a dollar or two. The fruit and vegetable vendors remain on the streets until perhaps 4 or 5 in the afternoon.

As soon as the first warm day arrives, possibly in April, *paleteros* appear, starting around noon, selling *paletas* (fruit ice bars), a treat available in all sorts of flavors. Paleteros show up near schools around lunchtime and return there at the end of the school day, when another stream of customers rushes out the doors. In the summer, paleteros walk the side streets and head for parks. As many as seven or eight of them may compete for business near a park.

For years, food vending on public ways was prohibited by city ordinance, so officials, including Alderman Muñoz, arrived at an informal agreement: as long as the carts were clean and the vendors did not obstruct the public way, police assigned to Little Village were to leave them alone. In 2015, however, the City of Chicago enacted an ordinance legalizing food peddlers but requiring them to buy a license, periodically have their carts inspected, and comply with food-preparation procedures, at a significant expense.

A parent picking up a child at Josefa Ortiz de Dominguez Elementary School, where a vendor peddles cotton candy at the end of the school day. Many children in Little Village walk home with their parent or guardian. (Photo by Philip Langdon)

"It just codified the ability of a more authoritarian alderman to shut folks down," said a skeptical Alderman Muñoz. Peddlers who wanted licenses obtained them, he said, but others who could not afford them asked him for leniency, and he agreed. Thus, the original Little Village understanding—that police are to let vendors operate unless they are causing trouble—remains in force in Little Village.

How much economic reward does a vendor reap? "I think people are forced to do that [operate a pushcart] when it's the last option," said Jaime di Paulo, executive director of the Little Village Chamber of Commerce. "For the vast majority, it's basically their last hope in terms of pursuing the American dream." Nearly a third of Little Village residents are poor, and peddling is a way of coping; it lets them earn some money despite a lack of formal education or understanding of English. Some people peddle year after year, into old age.

Maria Garcia, who arrived in Chicago in the late 1990s from Cuernavaca, south of Mexico City, illustrates how a determined person can use peddling as a stepping-stone. She made Mexican-style ice cream in her home, and for seven years, often with her sons Angel and Victor, she pushed an ice-cream cart through Little Village. "We would go all over the neighborhood," Victor Garcia told an interviewer.[7]

One of Maria Garcia's favorite spots was the sidewalk outside St. Agnes of Bohemia. The historically Czech parish turned predominantly Mexican American in the 1970s and today conducts nine Masses—two in English, the other seven in Spanish—each Sunday. On a typical Sunday, approximately four thousand people troupe in and out of St. Agnes. The church has no parking lot, so many parishioners walk to and from worship. Many of them stopped at her cart.

"Maria was a real hit. She had flavors you wouldn't find in stores— mango with chilies; pina colada; *elote* [corn]," Andrea Muñoz said. Elote-flavored ice cream became a best seller. The Garcias prided themselves on using high-quality natural ingredients and on using brown sugar rather than white sugar. People loved their concoction's light, refreshing quality that was closer to sorbet than to conventional ice cream.

Maria Garcia suffered a setback when someone reported her to the board of health, which does not allow people to make ice cream at home and sell it to the public, and her operation was shut down. The Garcias regrouped, however. They found a small retail building on Twenty-Seventh Street, fixed it up, and converted it into a coffee and ice-cream shop called Azucar, the Spanish word for sugar.

Word of mouth led customers to the shop, a cheerful little establishment that the Garcias outfitted with comfortable seating and clean, contemporary decor. Praise posted on sites like Yelp further boosted customer traffic. The key attraction was the shop's exceptional product, which the Garcias sold at very reasonable prices. By 2012, the

Maria Garcia and her son Victor serving customers at Azucar, their Mexican ice-cream shop on West Twenty-Seventh Street in Little Village. After several years of peddling ice cream on the streets, Mrs. Garcia opened the store, which enjoys a large following. (Photo by Philip Langdon)

Garcias—Maria still spoke only Spanish, but her sons had mastered both Spanish and English—were dispensing more than thirty flavors of ice cream. On weekends, people lined up out the door.

So, it is not unheard of for someone to advance from *ambulante* (cart pusher) to operator of a brick-and-mortar establishment. "People become entrepreneurs," said the chamber of commerce's di Paulo. If they do well, many of them want to expand, he said. "They feel they'd like to open a store."

Getting to Work

For much of the twentieth century, the Little Village neighborhood had factories close by. To the southeast lay a huge International Harvester plant. To the west, in Cicero, stood the 150-acre Hawthorne Works, which made telephone equipment for Western Electric. Many of the large employers are now gone. People seeking work have increasingly had to shift to public sector and service occupations in restaurants, hotels, landscaping, and other fields, many of which pay substantially less than factory work. Even so, many residents continue to work in manufacturing, mostly in smaller enterprises, and many of them some distance away.

A fourth of the workers who live in Little Village carpool to their jobs; the carpooling rate in this neighborhood is one of the highest in the city. Several day-labor offices operate in Little Village, and vans whisk the temporary workers off to small suburban factories. Some workers drive their own vehicles, although undocumented immigrants shy away from that for fear of being pulled over by police. Many ride buses. "Six bus lines crisscross the neighborhood, three going north–south, three east–west," Alderman Muñoz said. "The Cermak Road bus goes all the way to McCormick Place," North America's largest convention center, a major employer, he pointed out. "The Twenty-Sixth Street bus goes to Michigan and Randolph, the epicenter of downtown."

Little Village Organizers

Two individuals who have had a profound effect on the civic culture of Little Village are Marcos Muñoz and his wife, Andrea Muñoz. Marcos was born in Ciudad Acuna, Coahuila, a border town across the Rio Grande from Del Rio, Texas. In 1954, at age thirteen, Marcos left his hometown to find work in the United States and help feed his family.

As Andrea recounted, "He was hired to work on a farm in Texas, feeding animals, cleaning up behind them, collecting the eggs, et cetera. He slept in the barn with the animals. After six months he asked for his money so he could go back home—hoping he would have enough to buy a cart that he could use to sell fruits to help support his family.

"The rancher told him he could give it to him the next morning, and his wife would take him to the bus station in town to go back home. At 4:30 the next morning, he was wakened by immigration officials putting handcuffs on him. He asked to knock on the door of the rancher to get his money. There was no answer. He was deported back to Mexico."

He never did get paid. Marcos Muñoz nonetheless returned to the southwestern United States as a migrant worker, and in 1965, he met Cesar Chavez, who was organizing laborers in the vineyards of California. In 1967, Chavez sent Marcos to Boston to orchestrate the New England segment of a national boycott of table grapes, and there he met Andrea O'Malley, a teacher who had grown up in Brockton, Massachusetts, a shoe-manufacturing city south of Boston. Andrea quit her job to work on the boycott, the two wed, and after several years, the United Farm Workers transferred them to Chicago. That is how they came to live in Little Village in 1975.

Marcos, whose schooling had ended on the second day of second grade, got a job in a factory that made punch presses. Andrea became an immigration consultant for Catholic Charities and later rose through the Cook County Hospital system, directing the Dr. Jorge Prieto Family Health Center, among other responsibilities.

One day when Marcos was unemployed, he started sweeping the alley behind their house and managed to get neighbors to join him. The cleanup launched the Muñozes into years of organizing in Little Village. They established block clubs, some forty-five of them. Many residents were relatively new to the neighborhood, and some were new to the United States. They fared better when they learned from, and made common cause with, one another.

The Muñozes also became active in local politics, helping spark the careers of individuals such as Jesus "Chuy" Garcia, who in 1986 became Chicago's first Mexican American alderman. It was Garcia who forced Rahm Emanuel into a closely fought runoff election for mayor in 2015.

Of Chavez's legacy, Marcos said, "Cesar showed the importance of community."[a] Of Little Village residents, he said, "They're big contributors."

Andrea O'Malley Muñoz outside the house where she and her husband, Marcos—both former organizers for farmworker union leader Cesar Chavez—live in Little Village. The Muñozes have been involved in community causes since the 1970s. (Photo by Philip Langdon)

---

[a] Jason Pace, "The Legacy of Cesar Chavez and Marcos Munoz," *Uniting America* blog, Illinois Coalition for Immigrant and Refugee Rights, Mar. 27, 2013, http://icirr.org/content/legacy-cesar-chavez-and-marcos-munoz.

About one worker in six commutes via public transit, and another 7 percent—a respectable figure, said Scott Bernstein of the Chicago-based Center for Neighborhood Technology—walk to work. If you add those who work at home to those who walk to work, the combined group amounts to nearly 10 percent of the neighborhood's employed population. "This," Bernstein said, "reflects not only the obvious service jobs along the main shopping streets but also the service jobs at public facilities such as the schools and a still vibrant manufacturing sector—a shadow of its former self, but not all that far from the Stockyards Industrial District and the Central Manufacturing District."

The only rail service in Little Village is the Chicago Transit Authority's elevated Pink Line along the neighborhood's northern edge. It is a long trip, but some use it to head first toward downtown and then switch to a train to Chicago O'Hare International Airport, which is a huge job source. In addition, bicycling is growing, helped by the grid of streets and by bike routes and bike lanes established in recent years.

Pursuing Community Causes

Like the Czechs before them, Mexican residents in Little Village have established dozens of community organizations. Some are permanent, and others are targeted toward shorter-term goals. Schools, and school overcrowding, have ranked high among the residents' concerns.

"When I graduated from eighth grade in 1979, my math class was in a hallway," said Alderman Muñoz. "In 1993, it was *still* in a hallway. I made it my mission to argue for more schools. It was a community concern that I put on steroids." As a result, four new elementary schools and one middle school opened in the next five years. Those schools still look good today. Partly because they are embedded in a walkable neighborhood, many parents can be seen accompanying their children on foot to and from school each day. A further boost to education was the opening of the new Little Village Lawndale High School in 2005.

A key element in the neighborhood's progress has been the Little Village Community Development Corporation, now called Enlace Chicago. In 1999, when Jesus "Chuy" Garcia was hired as its first executive director, it was a small organization focused on creating a community-driven process for redevelopment of an abandoned industrial park at the western end of the Twenty-Sixth Street commercial district. Under Garcia, who had been the city's first Mexican American alderman and then Illinois's first Mexican American state senator, the organization expanded in size and scope. By the time Garcia stepped down in 2008, Enlace had 27 full-time employees and 120-part time staff members; it was pursuing a range of economic development initiatives and was countering gang violence, helping improve student achievement and graduation rates, and advocating for new parks and recreational spaces. As Little Village's largest community organization, Enlace led in-depth initiatives like the ones that produced a Little Village Quality of Life Plan in 2005 and a follow-up plan in 2013.

Gardens, Parks, Air, and Transit

Enlace Chicago, the Little Village Environmental Justice Organization (LVEJO), and other groups have converted parcels of disused land into community gardens. One basic purpose of the gardens is beautification. "This was a very ugly zone," said Maria Herrera, sitting in a garden near Twenty-Sixth Street, one of four gardens supported by Enlace. Herrera, who worked as a nurse in Mexico, spends much of the summer in that garden, helping people learn to grow vegetables, including plants native to Mexico. The gardeners learn about soils and fertilization and also become more knowledgeable about nutrition and health, including how to avoid becoming diabetic, an important matter for Latinos in the United States, who are about twice as likely as non-Hispanic whites to be afflicted with diabetes. Children play in the garden's small pool.

Maria Herrera, facilitator of community gardens for Enlace Chicago, in one of Enlace's gardens. She was a nurse in Mexico and helps Little Villagers learn about nutrition. (Photo by Philip Langdon)

"It's food access, it's household income generation, it's reviving from-scratch cooking," community organizer Alexander said about the gardens' varied value to the neighborhood. In a community where obesity is a problem that frequently leads to diabetes, the gardens are places that people can to walk to, thus encouraging physical activity. Women sit crocheting, sometimes while getting low-key, no-cost help with domestic or psychological problems. "We try to respond to mental health needs through informal social gathering spaces because it's really taboo to see a therapist," Alexander explained. "There's a lot of stigma around those kinds of needs. But," she noted, "a person can go to a garden" without being labeled a psychological client.

When the economy worsens, "the first thing to go from people's budgets is fruit and vegetables," said Kim Wasserman of LVEJO, showing off a garden her group created next to an industrial zone. For a yearly fee, participants have a place to tend raised beds, grow their own food, and have outdoor meals. "Every Wednesday," Wasserman said, "we eat what we grow."

"What does a healthy community look like?" Wasserman asks. "It has a mix of green space and industry and residential—not just one thing."

LVEJO and other groups fought for years to shut down the two old Fisk and Crawford coal-burning power plants, which had aggravated health problems such as asthma afflicting residents of Little Village and Pilsen. Protesters wore gas masks during Day of the Dead marches. A "Coalympics" got attention during Chicago's bid for an Olympics.[8] Finally, in 2012, both plants shut down, ending Chicago's dubious distinction of being the only major US city with two coal-fired plants operating within its borders.[9]

Little Village has had the smallest volume of open space per resident of any community in the city. At one point, it was a paltry 0.32 acre per inhabitant. Today it is 0.59 acre per resident—which is still a low figure, but it represents progress—and the community continues to push for more. One notable achievement was the 2014 opening of a new park, called La Villita, on twenty-two acres that had been polluted for decades by an asphalt roofing plant. Mayor Rahm Emanuel described the cleanup, carried out through the federal Superfund program, as "the largest brownfield conversion in America."[10] The site now boasts athletic fields, community gardens, basketball courts, a skate park, a children's playground, a picnic pavilion, and a multiuse trail with fitness stations, among other features.[11]

Wasserman noted that after the Little Village Lawndale High School was built on Thirty-First Street, the community relaunched a campaign to get the Chicago Transit Authority to establish a bus route on that thoroughfare.[12] Little Village Lawndale was the only high school in

The creation of twenty-two-acre La Villita Park on formerly contaminated industrial land was a victory for the Little Village Environmental Justice Organization
and for the community, which historically had a shortage of public green space.
La Villita, on South Sacramento Avenue in the southeast section of Little Village,
opened in December 2014. (Leslie Schwartz Photography)

Chicago that did not have a bus line within two blocks. At first, the
requests for buses on Thirty-First Street went nowhere. So, the youth
started working with local college students and LVEJO interns to craft
a bus proposal that articulated the need from a planning perspective—
encompassing infrastructure, walkability, ridership, and revenue. They
studied the business background of Chicago Transit Authority board
members and learned to speak their language.

A bus line, LVEJO noted, would reduce carbon dioxide emissions.
It would also help overcome a racial problem: African American students were being attacked while walking from the high school to a
distant spot where they boarded a bus that would take them home to
North Lawndale. Based on the group's report, the CTA agreed to a

one-hundred-eighty-day trial of half the proposed route. "That proved so successful that in 2012 the CTA made it permanent," Wasserman said. "In 2016 the second half of the route was approved."

The route attracts plenty of riders. "In the summer, the bus goes all the way to the lakefront," Wasserman pointed out. "Now you can get to the lake in 30 minutes instead of two hours." She draws inspiration from social protest movements in Mexico and said of her organization, "We see a long-term commitment to fight for what is right. We come from a country where organizing is part of our life."

Gang Violence

In *Great American City: Chicago and the Enduring Neighborhood Effect*, Harvard professor Robert J. Sampson leads readers through one of the most meticulous sociological examinations ever made of Chicago's neighborhoods. Research by Sampson and colleagues concludes that the city's Latino neighborhoods and immigrant neighborhoods generally function well. Latinos are blessed with a large array of organizations that help them deal with the challenges of urban life. Latinos, and immigrants as a whole, engage in less violence than do Chicagoans overall. As Sampson wrote, "Cities of concentrated immigration are some of the safest places around."[13]

That generalization is undercut by a rash of gang shootings and killings that has disturbed Chicago in recent years, some of them committed by young Latinos. In Little Village, the biggest threats are posed by the Latin Kings, who claim the east side of the neighborhood as their turf, and the Two Six Nation (named for Twenty-Sixth Street), who claim the west.[14] When the two gangs battle each other, sometimes bystanders are inadvertently killed.

Street gangs in Chicago can be traced as far back as violent white immigrant groups prior to the Civil War.[15] It was harassment of Latinos by non-Hispanic whites, some say, that led Latinos to form their own

gangs.[16] Once Latino organizations began attacking one another, a cycle
of violence and retribution was set in motion.

Territory is central to gang life. South Ridgeway Avenue, a largely residential street that runs north–south through the center of Little Village,
has at times functioned as the dividing line between the Latin Kings
and the Two Sixes, although when strongly challenged, the boundary
can shift. In 2013, according to Chicago police, the border was South
Hamlin Avenue, a block west of Ridgeway.[17] Members repeatedly tag
buildings on the border with gang initials and insignia and with insults
aimed at rivals. A three- or five-pointed crown announces that the area
is claimed by Latin Kings, and a bunny with a bent ear asserts that it is
the domain of the Two Six Nation.

Gangs can operate in many different settings, from suburban cul-
de-sacs to public housing towers. In Chicago, gangs have a geographi-
cal and hierarchical structure and are organized down to the street and
block level. When members tag a site, they may mark it with the name
of the street that is home to their subgroup. To control a territory, members may be ordered to walk their street for a set time—from, say, 9 in
the evening until 1 in the morning—said the Reverend Tom Boharic,
a young priest at St. Agnes of Bohemia who has made it his mission
to provide boys with alternatives to gang life. Gang members threaten
individuals who, purposely or inadvertently, are found wearing colors
of an opposing gang: black and gold for the Latin Kings, and black and
beige for the Two Sixes.

Electronic communication has introduced subtle changes in how
gang turf is defended. A young woman interviewed about territorial
conflicts in Little Village explained: "A decade ago, to gangbang was to
literally stand on your block, wearing your flag. Today, with more access
to technology and other outlets, physical confrontation at the border
is less frequent. Much of the border mentality is taken to the Internet." The Internet, however, ultimately leads back to confrontations in

physical places. The young woman pointed out that "when both sides meet in person, the clash is immediate and aided by guns."[18]

Violence is not random; rather, it is directed at specific individuals or groups, especially members of rival gangs. In her years of living and working in Little Village, Enlace Chicago's Alexander has never been attacked. "Mostly," she said, "being a white woman gives me a free pass." What matters most is whether a person fits into one of the ethnic or racial categories that a gang is intent on controlling. "My husband, who is Cuban, will not walk anywhere," Alexander said. "It's much more difficult to be a Latino male. You can't cross certain boundaries." Still, anyone can accidentally become a casualty if a gang fight erupts nearby. "People in general understand that they could catch a stray bullet," Alexander said.

Boundaries begin to constrain a Latino boy's movement when he is in fifth or sixth grade; that is the age at which boys start to be recruited by gangs. Little Village Lawndale High School was built with the intention of cutting across racial lines; the school encourages blacks and Latinos to avoid stereotyping and to instead become comfortable with each other. Although some progress has been made, blacks do not hang out much in Little Village after school and on weekends. Latino gangs make them feel unwelcome. In early 2009, young blacks were hurt in a series of violent incidents. Along the northern edge of Piotrowski Park, east of the school, Latino adults attacked African American students after they had left the school grounds. Some were injured badly enough to be hospitalized. Chicago Tenth District Police Commander Roberto Zavalo said some people in the neighborhood around the school assumed that the African American students were gang members, whether that was true or not. Whenever students display gang emblems in school, on that day "we're going to have a problem on 31st Street," Zavalo said.[19]

Why do boys in Little Village join gangs? Rarely is drug-selling the reason. The crucial thing about a gang is its ability to answer a teenage boy's desire for pride and reassurance; the gang affirms his identity and provides an outlet for demonstrating masculinity. Boys join a gang to feel valued and important. "They look for community, and that's where they find it," said Chicago historian Dominic Pacyga. "If a kid doesn't do well in school or do sports, some of them look to the streets," said Matt DeMateo, pastor of New Life Community Church. Part of the appeal of gangs has to with "just a lack of options," DeMateo said.

Pressure to join a gang seems particularly intense for those struggling to balance two contending cultures: the largely traditional Mexican culture of parents and grandparents and the fluid, impersonal, and sometimes hard-edged American culture that the rising generation ultimately has to adapt to. The tragedy is that gangs impart destructive lessons and promote behavior that is fundamentally hostile and hollow. Alexander described it this way: "Violence has to do with maintaining territory through peacocking, through strutting."

Establishing Order

If the neighborhood grid can be useful to gangs, the grid also functions in the reverse direction: the street, block, and building network helps residents resist gang incursions. A pattern of streets, sidewalks, and small front yards and of buildings punctuated by windows and doors that overlook the public realm makes it easy for people to notice troubling behavior and take action. Civility is reinforced by the large number of people walking to local destinations; by the influence of the corner stores; by the numerous street vendors; by the sprinkling of home businesses, alley mechanics, and other small enterprises throughout; and by institutions embedded in the neighborhood.

Through block clubs, Little Villagers exert collective responsibility for the safety and attractiveness of their surroundings. In many front yards there are simple globe lamps, installed by block club members years ago to illuminate the area and make the block safer stand. On some blocks, residents have painted the trunks of trees, a custom imported from Mexico; the whitened trunks reflect light from the globe lamps and from streetlights. Illumination was not the only reason for painting the tree trunks. Another aim, said Andrea Muñoz, was "to show others that the block was organized and united." The street grid, when it is intelligently cared for, sends messages, and these messages result in a more secure place to live.

After a group of neighbors has completed a block improvement, whether it is cleaning an alley, installing lighting, or painting the tree trunks, they often celebrate by having a block party. Jesus Garcia, born in the Mexican state of Durango and brought up mainly in Chicago, said, "Mexicans are a party culture—we have parties for everything. With children, there's always birthdays. There's loud music playing. There are smells from cooking. Guys being festive is normal—normal to us." Block clubs and the layout of the neighborhood allow these gregarious instincts to be channeled into community building.

Neighbors who see gang members hanging out down the block are encouraged to go out, act in a friendly manner, and ask "How are you doing?" said Andrea Muñoz. Neighbors get on their phones and prod other neighbors to come out, too. The aim is to start a conversation. The gang members may then decide to move to another location—sometimes that is the most that can be hoped for—but there is always the chance that a better long-term relationship will develop.

Multiple organizations fight back against gang graffiti defacing buildings in the neighborhood. Municipal crews often spray brown paint over gang tags. That solution is better than letting graffiti accumulate, but it is not ideal. Who wants to see the bottom 6 feet of apartment buildings covered in drab brown paint? The Reverend Tom Boharic of St. Agnes of Bohemia sees the city paint jobs as a "ghetto blaster" approach that overcomes the problem only temporarily.

Some community groups instead replace graffiti with paintings that will have a more lasting and positive effect than the city's solution.

Little Village abounds with tall street trees. Some of them have had their trunks painted white, a custom from Mexico that was adopted by some of Little Village's block clubs, in part to herald that the neighbors are organized. (Photo by Philip Langdon)

The Reverend Tom Boharic of St. Agnes of Bohemia Catholic Church in front of a mural that students under his instruction painted at South Avers Avenue and West Twenty-Seventh Street, not far from the border between the Latin Kings and the Two Six gang. (Photo by Philip Langdon)

Father Tom runs Imago Dei, a program that brings together boys in the fifth through eighth grades (and sometimes higher grades) and authorizes them to paint murals over the gang tags. The boys' creations range from traditional Mexican-style murals to contemporary art. "We put up a Unity mural representing the unity of cultures," Father Tom said as he walked the blocks near his church, touring the boys' artwork. Murals with religious themes stand a good chance of remaining undisturbed. "Even the gangs are religious," he said. "They'll tag on any building but never on a church." Father Tom noted that the community likes the murals created by youths he supervises. "People will congratulate them on the work," he said.

In a few instances, the community has taken sites notorious for violence and turned them into neighborhood assets. That happened to a

A walk home from school includes passing one of the many religious murals painted on garage doors and other surfaces in Little Village. The inscription translates to, "Rise up, my son, and go in peace." (Photo by Philip Langdon)

parking lot at South Lawndale Avenue and West Thirty-First Street, next to Ortiz de Dominguez Elementary School and close to a gang border. Where teachers used to park their cars, a soccer field now echoes with the sounds of kids at play. Rob Castañeda cofounded a youth organization, Beyond the Ball, to reach out to young boys through sports. He did so despite great risk to himself and his family. In 1999 and 2000, gang members, sometimes carrying rifles, tried to force him out of the neighborhood. "They were breaking our windows," Castañeda said. "They set our house on fire." Yet Castañeda and his family stayed and made a growing impact. "By 2006," he said, "we were working with about 250 guys from the neighborhood. We saw the amazing culture we were building. The guys who attacked our house went to prison. Their kids are in our program."

One of the challenges in Little Village is that many parents work long hours or at more than one job, and many are not around when their children get out of school. Castañeda's program uses organized play to help fill that gap. "When people play," he observed, "it makes them more resistant to trauma."

Lessons of Little Village

Little Village has a fundamentally walkable character, perhaps not to the same degree as the intimately scaled rowhouse neighborhoods in Center City Philadelphia, but Little Villagers can accomplish a great deal on foot. The community's density and pedestrian-oriented uses benefit residents in multiple ways: by lessening their need for automobiles, reducing their transportation expenses, making the neighborhood more self-sufficient, and helping people form bonds with their neighbors.

Stores and services of nearly every kind, including health clinics, professional offices, and food banks, are within walking distance. Businesses specializing in Mexican products, from cooking ingredients to *quinceañera* dresses, have become regional attractions, generating jobs and income and reinforcing local pride.

Despite its strengths, the Twenty-Sixth Street corridor cries out for physical improvement. Outdated or harsh facades need to be upgraded, as Jaime Di Paulo of the Little Village Chamber of Commerce is quick to acknowledge. Visual appeal may not be the first thing that newly arrived immigrants worry about, but in the long run, the look of a place does matter. Americans' standards for the built environment have risen tremendously in recent years. People are drawn to urban business districts that have a lively or uplifting spirit and are disappointed when that spirit is missing. A thoroughfare like Twenty-Sixth Street will fare better if it compares favorably to other neighborhood business districts in Chicago and the suburbs. Little Village merchants should take a lesson from the success of Maria Garcia's little Azucar ice-cream shop on Twenty-Seventh Street, where not

A High School Born of a Hunger Strike

When Chicago school officials put plans for a promised Little Village high school on hold, claiming financial difficulties, the neighborhood did what it often does: it turned to collective action. Block club leaders who had been trained in community organizing began a series of events that culminated in a highly effective protest. On May 13, 2001, Mother's Day, fifteen Mexican American mothers and grandmothers pitched tents on the school site on Little Village's southwestern industrial edge, named their settlement "Camp Cesar Chavez," and began a hunger strike.

"Every night, different churches would take the lead, marching to support them," said Andrea Muñoz. The protesters were upset that the board of education had recently opened two selective-enrollment high schools in more affluent white areas of the city yet had postponed constructing a high school in Little Village. After nineteen days of subsisting on broth, water, and Gatorade, the protesters achieved their goal and brought the strike to an end on June 1. Mayor Richard M. Daley replaced two of the top leaders of the board of education and on June 26 appointed Arne Duncan the new chief executive officer of Chicago Public Schools.[a] Duncan, later secretary of education in the Obama administration, gave the community a crucial financial commitment, and in the fall of 2005, the Little Village Lawndale High School opened on South Kostner Avenue at West Thirty-First Street.

The protesters "not only insisted on being a significant part of the planning process, but also came to guide it," Joanie Friedman wrote in a history of the controversy.[b] Urban high schools tend to be large, impersonal institutions, but Duncan "said kids function better in a small school, where teachers know the kids," Muñoz recalled. Thus, it was decided that the new high school, designed for approximately 1,600 students, would consist of four small, autonomous academies in one building. The four discrete parts are connected by a central atrium. Each academy has its own principal and teaching staff, but some facilities, including the library, swimming pool, auditorium, and health center, are shared.

Advocates of the new school were allowed to work with architects to

---

[a] Ana Beatriz Cholo, "Little Village Getting School It Hungered For," *Chicago Tribune*, Feb. 27, 2015, http://articles.chicagotribune.com/2005-02-27/news /0502270311-1-hunger-strike-chicago-public-schools-chief-arne-duncan.

[b] Joanie Friedman, "Contested Space," *AREA Chicago*, http://areachicago.org/contested-space/; first published as "Contested Space: The Struggle for the Little Village Lawndale High School," in *Critical Planning Journal* 14 (Summer 2007): 143–56.

ensure that the culture of the community and the memory of the strike were reflected in the building and grounds. Public charrettes (intensive design sessions) were convened to learn what was important to the community. The architects distributed cameras to residents and asked them to capture images that defined the neighborhood. Participants returned with images of local murals, monuments, and mosaics, which the architects then incorporated into the building design.

"The school was a symbolic victory for the neighborhood," Muñoz said. Testifying to that, one of the academies is the School for Social Justice, which keeps people aware of the struggle and the ideals of the strikers. Enrollment boundaries for the $63 million complex were set so that the student body would be integrated, with approximately 70 percent Latino students (largely from Little Village) and approximately 30 percent African American students (overwhelmingly from North Lawndale).

Mural in a corridor of Social Justice High School, one of the four autonomous schools that make up the Little Village Lawndale High School Campus on South Kostner Avenue. The inscription says: "Hope is believing in spite of the evidence and then watching the evidence change." (Photo by Philip Langdon)

only is the product appealing and reasonably priced; the atmosphere is artful and inviting.

Public transit in Little Village is decent and well-used. It would be even more valuable if the buses ran more frequently and to more destinations.

More parks, community gardens, and green spaces are needed. Alderman Muñoz is correct when he describes the scarcity of parks as a problem inherited from decades ago. The businesspeople who developed industry, commerce, and housing in South Lawndale a century or more ago did not reserve enough land for public enjoyment. The community is making progress—inserting gardens and play areas into vacant spaces, converting disused industrial land into parks when opportunities arise, and preparing for the Paseo, a 4-mile biking and walking path that when completed will provide an enjoyable off-road connection between Little Village and Pilsen.[20] The more these kinds of projects are carried out, the healthier and steadier the neighborhood will be.

Vigorous organizations that focus on neighborhood well-being are one of Little Village's strengths. The energy displayed by these organizations and their members has been impressive.

Gang violence is probably the biggest single threat to Little Village's long-term stability. Wholesale migration from Mexico to the United States appears to be over for the immediate future, and to be sustainable, Little Village will have to hold on to a large proportion of its existing residents, not lose them to suburbs or other sections of the city. That will be difficult unless gang violence is reduced. To their credit, community organizers realize that gangs pose a serious challenge. The gang problem leads back to families and schools. If some families cannot steer their boys clear of gangs, schools and outside organizations will have to work extra hard to see that boys follow a productive path. The rate of high school graduation, worrisomely low, must somehow be substantially raised.

On the whole, it is heartening to see how well Little Village is doing.

Residents building composting bins in a community park organized by the Little Village Environmental Justice Organization. Community gardens grow food, aid nutrition, and bring Little Village residents together. (Photo courtesy of Little Village Environmental Justice Organization)

Says Michael Rodriguez, a former leader of Enlace Chicago, "For Mexican Americans, this is where you get your foothold."

"Foothold" is an apt word choice, because Little Village is a place where people put their feet to good use. They walk. The walkability of this section of Chicago, home to immigrants and the children of immigrants for much of its history, reinforces the community's cohesiveness and serves its residents well.

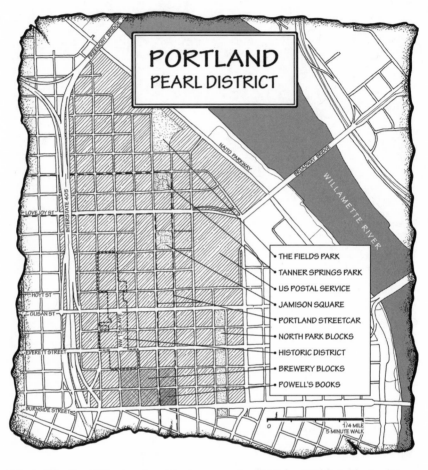

Map of the Pearl District, showing the network of 200-by-200-foot blocks that was extended northward across the former rail yards. A thirteen-acre tract west of NW Broadway is a US Postal Service Center that is expected to be redeveloped with commercial and residential buildings, including an estimated six hundred affordable apartments. (Drawing by Dhiru A. Thadani)

CHAPTER 5

Redeveloping with Pedestrians in Mind: The Pearl District, Portland, Oregon

In 1992, the *Atlantic Monthly* sent me to Portland, Oregon, to find out how that city, in a span just short of twenty years, had turned a run-of-the-mill downtown into one most appealing in the nation. At that time, the city's population had risen to 446,000 and was growing nearly 20 percent per decade, and Portland was on its way to becoming the star of American urban planning.[1]

A six-lane expressway on the west bank of the Willamette River had been torn out and replaced by thirty-six acres of parkland, reconnecting the city center to the waterfront. A parking garage in the heart of downtown had been razed to make way for Pioneer Courthouse Square, an amphitheater-like space accommodating all sorts of outdoor activities, from festivals and musical performances to protests and people-watching. The first line of MAX, the metropolitan light-rail transit system, had begun transporting thousands of suburbanites into downtown, not just Monday through Friday but on the weekends, too, when the well-kept city center became the region's living room.

Looking south into the Pearl District in 1997, when much of it was still a working rail yard. Two years later, the Lovejoy Viaduct in the middle of this view was demolished and replaced by Lovejoy Street, now a principal east–west route across the Pearl. (Photo courtesy of BruceForsterPhotography.com)

Although my focus was on downtown, a few Portlanders drew my attention to a district just north of it. A several-block area north of Burnside Street, part of district known historically as the Northwest Industrial Triangle, had been rechristened the "Pearl District" in 1986 by Thomas Augustine, owner of an art gallery there. He had coined the name because he saw the area, which was dominated by large old warehouses, as being like a crusty oyster: rough on the outside, but holding pearls within. The "pearls" were artist studios, lofts, and galleries, which took up growing portions of the rugged warehouses. Artists and their followers were moving to the warehouses because rents were cheap and there was a cluster of people with shared interests: potters, painters, sculptors, graphic artists, photographers, set builders, and so on.[2]

"It was a dormant industrial area," recalled Al Solheim, an investor who loved "great old buildings." Warehouses two to eight stories tall, constructed mainly of brick and timber, had been erected in the first two decades of the 1900s as storage for manufacturers. Railroad tracks ran down NW Twelfth, Thirteenth, and Fifteenth Avenues, allowing freight cars to rumble up to the loading docks of companies like Crane, the plumbing fixture manufacturer, and Maytag, the washing machine maker.

In the decades after World War II, manufacturers cast off multistory warehouses as obsolete. Moving and storage companies acquired many of the buildings, but by the 1970s, even the moving companies had little use for them. Solheim believed that the buildings could have a future. His modus operandi was that he would buy a warehouse for very little money and convert it to self-storage units (a profitable enterprise both then and now) or space for artistic enterprises. The big, open floors would be subdivided. "Very few artists need 10,000 square feet. They need 500 to 1,500 feet," Solheim said. He partitioned the interior, installed up-to-date fire and life-safety systems, and brought in artists and galleries. He did that from the mid-1980s onward, keeping the rents low enough that artists could remain there for years.

Meanwhile, on the north side of Burnside Street, the crosstown traffic artery that separated the Pearl from downtown, Michael Powell and his father, Walter Powell, converted inexpensive buildings into a bookstore. From a small start in 1971, they developed Powell's City of Books into the largest new-and-used bookseller in the United States. By the 1980s, the store filled an entire bock.

West of Powell's was a brewery named Blitz-Weinhard that made beer in a hodgepodge of buildings constructed shortly after 1900. A few light industries also operated in the district. In the northeast sector lay acre after acre of rail yard, most of it moribund. Things were stirring, but on the whole, said Michael Powell, the area from Burnside Street northward was "an undeveloped neighborhood—mostly warehouses, wholesalers, and auto repair shops."[3]

The Pearl District Today

Since the 1970s, the Pearl District has grown from the old warehouse area to encompass about 120 blocks, from Burnside Street north to the river and from Broadway west to Interstate 405. In that time, it has become the best large, walkable urban neighborhood created in the core of an American city.

Many things that gave the district its character decades ago are still present. With support from developers, a preservation district was established along several blocks of NW Thirteenth Avenue, the spine of the warehouse area. The buildings have since been converted to a mix of uses, including loft apartments, offices, stores, restaurants, and galleries. A warehouse from 1908 became headquarters for the international advertising firm Wieden + Kennedy. Microsoft, Adidas, the Keen shoe company, the McCormick & Schmick's restaurant chain, and other businesses have opened offices in the Pearl. Most buildings in the district, new or old, have uses at street level that catch the eyes of pedestrians passing by.

People from all over the United States trek to Powell's, where 365 categories of books—one million volumes in all—are shelved in high-ceilinged rooms with concrete floors. More than a dozen art galleries operate in the Pearl, which is home to two arts educational institutions: the Pacific Northwest College of Art and the Art Institute of Portland. The biggest cluster of retail is on or near Burnside Street, but small stores are scattered throughout the district, and there are three grocery stores: Safeway, Whole Foods Market, and World Foods.

Sparsely populated in the early 1990s, the Pearl now has 7,000 residents. Most are middle class, some of them transplants from other cities. For example, Richard and Vicky Hahn told me that they had examined

Boston, Philadelphia, Denver, and Seattle as potential places to settle in before choosing Portland for its mild climate, first-rate transit, reasonable cost of living, and urban qualities.

A significant portion of the district's housing is reserved for low- and moderate-income residents. One modest-income resident, Jeff Nelson, told me that cancer had devoured his savings, forced him to quit working, and caused him to look for a government-assisted apartment. "I hit it lucky," he said about finding housing in the Pearl. Another tenant, whose mental problems and use of alcohol and drugs had ended his employment, acknowledged, "I have to pay the piper now." Of the building he lives in and of the Pearl in general, he said, "This is a good place to be." Yet another tenant, Stephen Roberts, in his sixties, who once owned a water-testing business, said he is pleased by the Pearl's "sense of community" and its inclusion of people who would have difficulty paying market rates for housing. "Your neighborhood is made safe because the person next door is of good character, not because they have money," he said.

Steve Rudman, former executive director of Home Forward, Portland's public housing authority, said many of the renters in subsidized housing are "service workers, people who work in the restaurants" and in other jobs that pay modestly. He explained, "Because most of the subsidized buildings are handsome, not drab, many visitors think the Pearl is richer than it is." Most people, when they walk down the street, "won't realize there are poor people there," said Rudman.

"What I love about the Pearl is that it's a real neighborhood," said Barbara Berman, who lives with her husband in a condo four blocks north of Burnside Street. "We walk everywhere. There are three movie theaters within walking distance. There are three theaters for plays. There are more restaurants than I could tell you." Patricia Gardner, a leader of the Pearl District Neighborhood Association, said her husband was surprised and pleased by the Pearl after previously living in Forest

Park, a large-lot, semirural area on Portland's northwest edge. "There's so much more community," Gardner said. "You know your neighbors. So many people are out walking."

A Pathbreaking Agreement

Redevelopment of the Pearl was a local effort. "We had a good planning bureau, good infrastructure people, no corruption," Solheim said. "We had a half-dozen really good local developers, people who put their offices down here." Two of the early ones were Pat Prendergast and John Carroll, who in 1990 acquired forty acres of rail yards previously owned by Burlington Northern Railroad. They formed a company called Hoyt Street Properties to erect buildings on their land and gradually sell the properties off.

The potential of the district was first seriously examined in 1983, when the American Institute of Architects assembled a Regional/Urban Design Assistance Team to come up with ideas for the area. In the years that followed, other organizations weighed in, and there was extensive public discussion. In 1994, Portland's city council adopted the River District Development Plan, which called for a high-density, mixed-use "community of neighborhoods" in the Pearl District and Old Town/ Chinatown, including two thousand to three thousand new housing units on the rail yards. That was a remarkable ambition for a city where few people were accustomed to high density.

Preservation of many of the warehouses and creation of parks and recreational areas were two important parts of the evolving vision. The city and Hoyt Street Properties proposed a development agreement outlining what things the developer would do for the city and what the city, in return, would do to make the development successful. One idea was to have the public sector install a streetcar line linking the Pearl more strongly to the rest of the city's core. Carroll liked that idea and even went to Europe to visit streetcar manufacturers.

Ownership of Hoyt Street Properties changed, and the city-developer agreement did not come about until Homer Williams, who had been a developer in Portland's West Hills, became the lead figure in the company in the mid-1990s. Williams, an unpretentious man known for his "minimum-wage wardrobe," got along well with the three-term mayor, Vera Katz. "Homer's got a holistic view of the universe," Katz once said. "Our conversations are usually about bigger issues, demographics and how the city is changing."[4] Williams saw potential where other people mostly saw problems. "You need to figure out what the public benefit of a project is," Williams explained. "If you can't figure that out, you're finished."

Williams remained at the company only a few years, but during that time, he saw Hoyt through two years of intensive negotiations about what would be built on the rail yards, how dense the development would be, how high buildings would rise, what transportation improvements would be needed, how many parks would be created, and how much of the housing would be affordable. The result, in 1997, was a painstakingly detailed agreement.

"We felt there was a movement back into cities," Williams said. "We felt there was chance of it happening in Portland, and this would be an opportunity for the city to reinvent itself." City Hall wanted density, but along with that, it wanted the makeup of the neighborhood to reflect the economic makeup of the city. Hoyt agreed that 35 percent of the housing the company created would be for people of moderate, low, or extremely low income, households whose income was no more than 80 percent of the area's median family income and in many cases much less.[5]

S. Bruce Allen, who worked for the Portland Development Commission as the city's lead negotiator in Pearl redevelopment, said that early in the process, "there was a general consensus about the need to have a mix of affordable housing at various income levels, as that direction came from the city council. It stuck! The housing advocates got much of what they wanted."

Ed McNamara, an affordable-housing developer, said that the council in fact was responding to a campaign by an extremely persistent group: the Portland Organizing Project, a band of citizens that used strategies formulated by Saul Alinsky's Industrial Areas Foundation in Chicago. The group, supported by churches, focused on social justice issues such as reducing the disparity between local housing costs, which were soaring in the mid-1990s, and local wages, which were barely rising. The *Catholic Sentinel* said that the Organizing Project tried to "counter the tendency for citizens to be identified as merely 'market share.'"[6]

Dick Harmon, who trained Organizing Project members, said that when the group learned that the city had authorized a River District task force to chart the future of the Pearl and a low-income area directly to the east (together officially known as the River District), they did research on task force participants, on who owned land or held mortgages in the River District, and on which task force participants had contributed money to the campaigns of city council members. The group put together a document detailing those financial ties, but did not release it to the press. Instead, Harmon said, the Organizing Project used its findings as a negotiating tool. "The city council understood that if we went public with this document, there would be hell to pay," he said.

Members of the Organizing Project also met with Portland's business establishment to persuade business leaders that the city did in fact have an affordability problem. The outcome was that the city allocated $24 million for affordable housing, much of it in the River District, and got Hoyt to agree that 35 percent of the housing on Hoyt's land would be affordable. Through a tax-increment financing (TIF) mechanism, the city devoted 30 percent of the district's growth in property tax revenue to the support of affordable housing. In 1998, the city established a River District urban renewal district to shepherd public investment into the Pearl and adjacent Old Town/Chinatown.

Under the city-developer contract, when the city built a park or started to install the streetcar line, Hoyt had to produce a higher density of housing development on part of the company's land. When the first park was built, the required density rose by twenty-two units an acre. The quid pro quo meant a bigger profit for Hoyt, more revenue for the city, and a more robust neighborhood—more residents, more businesses, and more eyes on the street. In 1997, however, the Pearl was not yet a proven location for concentrated development, especially for condominiums, which were a significant part of the development package. "It was a time in our city when none of this kind of housing had been built," recalled Tiffany Sweitzer, who did much of Hoyt's negotiating with the city and later became the company's president.

As it turned out, people were quick to move into the Pearl, and the greater density "created a lot of the success of this neighborhood," Sweitzer said. Hoyt's first four buildings were only four to five stories; the maximum allowable height was 75 feet. As time went by, Hoyt was permitted to go up to 125 feet and then higher. By 2016, outright height restrictions had been eliminated in the Pearl; the only limit was the floor-area ratio: 9 square feet of interior space for every 1 square foot of land. The ratio had started at 2 to 1, but over the years it had more than quadrupled.

Linked Parks

Hoyt and the City of Portland eventually agreed that three parks totaling about five acres would be built between Tenth and Eleventh Avenues, each with a different character. All three would be linked, in landscape architect Peter Walker's design, by a boardwalk of ipe, a durable tropical wood. Today, the southernmost park, Jamison Square, is a lively gathering place where water flows through a grouping of square rocks; on warm summer days, children splash in its shallow pool.[7]

Three blocks north of Jamison Square is Tanner Springs Park, a quiet, naturalistic environment where people stroll, practice yoga, picnic, and enjoy a serene atmosphere. Designer Herbert Dreiseitl worked

The fountain and wading pool have made Jamison Square, one of a sequence of three parks created in the Pearl District, extremely popular with children. (Photo by Philip Langdon)

at perfecting the sound made by the park's rushing water. Another two blocks north lies the three-acre Fields Park, which features a large grassy oval where people play volleyball, fly kites, toss Frisbees, and gather for events like the Portland Craft Beer Festival. The park presents dramatic views of the Fremont Bridge over the Willamette River, and it has a dog park, popular with the Pearl's many canine owners.

At the eastern edge of the Pearl, close to Old Town, are the North Park Blocks, five blocks of green space created in the nineteenth century. Over the decades, the North Park Blocks have gone through cycles of decay and revival, and recently the park blocks sparked controversy when they were occupied by homeless people. How to manage those blocks remains in question.

The atmosphere varies greatly from one part of Jamison Square to another. This view, capturing the park's contrasts of shade and sun, looks toward the wading pool. (Photo by Philip Langdon)

The Viaduct and the Streetcar

The Lovejoy Viaduct, an ugly elevated road that carried cars and trucks across the northern part of the district, above the rail yards, had to be removed before people would be willing to live in the northern part of the Pearl. The viaduct came down in 1999, making way for development of a "main street" corridor along Lovejoy Street, where the ground floor was devoted to retail and housing was built on the upper floors. The corridor became a center of activity for the emerging community.

The required density on part of the former rail yards jumped to 109 units an acre when the Portland Streetcar line was built.[8] Despite critics who claimed that buses would be cheaper and more flexible than streetcars, officials believed that a streetcar—its route visible and permanent—would be essential, bringing people into a part of the Pearl they might otherwise have considered too distant.

The Portland Streetcar began operating in 2001, its sleek, low-floor vehicles (easy to enter and exit) running through the Pearl District to a hospital and retail/restaurant area several blocks west, on NW Twenty-Third Avenue; to downtown; and to Portland State University. As its route extended—first to a somewhat isolated waterfront area south of downtown and then across the Willamette to the Central Eastside— Williams marveled that "it turned into an economic engine." Between 1998 and 2015, land within a quarter-mile of the streetcar line experienced a development boom. Twenty-three million square feet of real estate were built, including 7.7 million square feet of commercial space and nearly eighteen thousand residential units. Economic analysts estimated that 35 percent of the commercial development and 41 percent of the housing construction was a result of the streetcar line being close by.[9] The number of people living in the corridor jumped by 34.9 percent, almost triple the 12.4 percent growth of the city as a whole.

Researchers found that nearly 39 percent of residents along the streetcar line did not own a car. In Portland as a whole, residents made 62

Neon-lit "Go by Streetcar" sign overlooks the Portland Streetcar route on NW Lovejoy Street. Development has boomed along the streetcar's route. (Photo by Philip Langdon)

percent of their trips in single-occupant vehicles, but residents within a quarter-mile of the streetcar tracks drove in single-occupant vehicles at a smaller rate, 43 percent. "The streetcar is the primary way I get

The five-block Brewery Blocks complex developed by Gerding Edlen includes some sections only three stories high; their low height helps make the setting comfortable for pedestrians. The development contains offices, housing, cultural activities, restaurants, and some of the district's most upscale retail establishments. (Photo courtesy of Gerding Edlen)

around," William Beers, a low-income tenant in his sixties, said. Mobility is crucial to Beers. "I have doctor issues," he said. "I use the streetcar and the tram to get to OHSU," a hospital at Oregon Health & Science University on Marquam Hill south of downtown.

"I pretty much manage my life along the streetcar," said Kate Washington, who moved into the Ramona, a subsidized building in the Pearl, in 2011 and rode the streetcar to Portland State to finish a bachelor's in sociology and earn a master's in urban planning. "It's easy to have a good, productive life here without using a car."

Rick Gustafson, who headed the nonprofit public benefit corporation that manages the Portland Streetcar, asserts that if people can satisfy all their needs within less than 2 miles, an automobile becomes the least favored way of getting around. If necessities are close to home, in mixed-use development, he said, "you might walk or bike or take transit."

The streetcar is not swift, but speed is rarely the goal of a streetcar line. The aim, in dense urban settings, is to act as a "walk extender," helping pedestrians cover more ground and reach more destinations than they could otherwise do in several minutes. There is another goal as well: creating a settlement pattern that reduces the burden on the natural environment.

The Secret Sauce: Small Blocks

In the nineteenth century, the core of Portland was laid out with small blocks, 200 feet on a side. By the standards of most US cities, 200-by-200-foot blocks are tiny, no more than a fourth the size of a typical block in New York City's Manhattan. The grid of small square blocks had never penetrated Portland's rail yards, so when the city and developers began to think about redevelopment, they looked at whether the small-block network should be extended. Bruce Allen at the Portland Development Commission saw advantages in small blocks. The downtown had functioned well under that system. Small blocks give pedestrians and motorists alike a greater choice of routes, on streets that are not so big and harried that they become dangerous or uncomfortable for walking. "It's so efficient for traffic," Allen said. The pattern of small blocks "allows people to get in and out quickly."

"We didn't want to follow the 200-by-200-foot grid," with its predominantly one-way, two-lane streets, said Sweitzer. "That was a major obstacle for us." Hoyt accepted a layout mostly of 200-foot blocks nonetheless. "It wasn't worth the fight," she said. Looking back, Homer Williams concurs. He now calls the 200-foot blocks "Portland's secret sauce," the thing that makes for "better human scale, more corners, dueling restaurants on the corners."

The width of the street from curb to curb is generally 36 feet, a distance most pedestrians can cover quickly, thus reducing their chance of being hit by a vehicle. Sidewalks, including the areas occupied by street trees, are usually 12 feet wide. The distance from building front to building front is 60 feet, which is small enough to give the street space a degree of enclosure. With traffic spread out over numerous streets, many intersections do not need traffic signals. A stop sign suffices, which is good, because pedestrians usually feel less threatened when crossing at a stop sign than at a traffic signal, where a motorist may speed up when trying to beat a changing light.

Parking is mostly on the street or underground. Even when the Blitz-Weinhard brewery closed in 1999 and its five blocks began being converted by Gerding Edlen into a seven-building assemblage of top-quality office space, upscale retail, and luxury condo towers called the Brewery Blocks, the parking—1,300 spaces in all—was placed underground.

The Pearl benefited from Portland's years of experiments in making the downtown welcoming to pedestrians. Downtown, the city had determined that ground floors of buildings should contain "active uses" such as retail, restaurants, and services. People passing by should be able to glimpse a building's interior. Buildings should not have back sides dominated by dumpsters and truck bays. Developers should make buildings presentable on all four exposures. Those standards were applied to the Pearl as well.

Not everything worked perfectly. Initially, retail "was an afterthought for us," Switzer at Hoyt Street Properties admitted. "We were so focused on getting the condo units sold." Windows of retail spaces were not as large as they should have been, and in some buildings, retail space remained vacant for a year or more. Gradually, however, everyone learned how to do better, incorporating more glass and designing ground-floor units flexibly so that they could function initially as residential or work space and be converted into stores or restaurants when

Midblock passages provide lushly landscaped shortcuts through many of the Pearl District's residential complexes. This one, designed by Koch Landscape Architects for Hoyt Street Properties' Bridgeport Condominiums and built in 2003, was the first midblock passage open to the public. (Photo courtesy of Steve Koch, Koch Landscape Architects)

the area's population grew. Municipal design review encouraged developers to look several years into the future.

The Pearl was devoid of trees until the 1970s, when property owners started to plant them. "Nothing transforms an area like artists and street trees," Al Solheim likes to say. Later the city mandated street trees. In a few places—such as stretches of Irving and Kearney Streets—profusely landscaped pedestrian passages were built rather than through streets for motor vehicles. These green passages offer people quiet places to sit or meet friends.

Art also arrived. In 2001, Kenny Scharf created fanciful 30-foot-tall aluminum totem poles—the Tikitotmoniki Totems—to cover a few of the catenary poles of the streetcar system and add to the area's charm. When plans were afoot to demolish the Lovejoy Viaduct, a citizens' group resolved to save some of the viaduct's stout concrete columns, part of the Pearl's quirky artistic inheritance. Athanasios Efthimiou "Tom" Stefopoulos, a Greek immigrant, railroad switchman, and master calligrapher, had painted depictions of Greek mythology, Americana, and Biblical imagery on the columns in the late 1940s and early 1950s.[10] People liked the Lovejoy Columns and insisted on not losing them, so two of the 29,000-pound columns were reinstalled in a plaza on NW Tenth Avenue, where they are focal points for celebrations of the district's history and culture.

Basic human needs were not forgotten. A modular public restroom, the Portland Loo, was designed under the city's auspices, and the sleek units were installed in locations near parks. "They're very popular and very clean," said Kate Washington. "Everybody who has a child is very grateful they're there."

Holding On to History

Many of the Pearl District's older buildings have been brought back to full use. Developer Gerding Edlen preserved the turreted First Regiment Armory Annex, built in 1891, converting the interior into a six-hundred-seat theater and installing state-of-the-art environmental features. The Romanesque Revival-style building, used chiefly for performances of Portland Center Stage, became the first building on the National Register of Historic Places to win LEED Platinum certification. It is part of Gerding Edlen's five-block, seven-building Brewery Blocks complex, which also saved the old Blitz-Weinhard brewhouse.

Close by on NW Eleventh Avenue, the two-story North Bank Depot buildings of the Spokane, Portland and Seattle Railway were converted by Prendergast & Associates into townhouses. The buildings featured elevated concrete loading docks along their fronts—survivals from

The Portland Loo, one of the much-appreciated twenty-four-hour public restrooms in the Pearl District. This one is at the edge of Jamison Square. (Photo by Philip Langdon)

One of the North Bank Depot buildings on NW Eleventh Avenue that was converted to townhouses. Loading docks that rise a few feet above street level now function as front porches. (Photo by Philip Langdon)

when the buildings functioned as a passenger rail station and as freight storage—that have been cleverly turned into front porches.[11]

On Thirteenth Avenue, loading docks on the fronts of warehouses became walkways. Their elevation a few feet above the street make them interesting places to stroll. Some loading docks have been used for outdoor dining. Most of the walking on Thirteenth Avenue occurs in the street. It is a "shared street," where pedestrians and slowly moving cars coexist. NW Thirteenth has become a popular place to hang out.

In its "Last Place in the Downtown Plan," prepared in 1983, the Design Assistance Team of the American Institute of Architects (AIA) proposed establishing a fifty-acre historic district in Portland. The historic district that the city ultimately authorized is smaller and covers approximately seven blocks. Thirty-five of the ninety historic buildings identified by the AIA had been respectfully renovated for new uses by 2008, but then came the global recession; as the pace of development began to pick up during the recovery, old buildings unprotected by historic designation were demolished. By the estimate of Rollins College professor Bruce Stephenson, twenty-five to thirty old buildings (some of them architecturally undistinguished) have been lost. "A lot of buildings are being taken down and being replaced by fifteen- to twenty-five-story apartments and condos," said Solheim. "It's a little distressing for someone who's been here as long as I have."

Affordability under Stress

Concern has been growing about whether housing costs in the Pearl may drive out people who do not qualify for subsidized units but are not affluent enough to pay the rents being charged for market-rate apartments. In the first condo building erected after the 2008 recession, the prices of units were breathtaking, averaging $700 per square foot.[12] The Pearl is attracting growing numbers of businesses that pay their employees generously. Wealthy people who are enthusiastic about urban living are also arriving. Together, these market forces are pushing up rents and sales prices and challenging the budgets of middle-income residents who want to remain in the Pearl. "Affordability is on the tip of everybody's tongue," Stephenson said.

Meanwhile, affordable housing production in the Pearl has not been as high as anticipated. In the first fifteen years after Hoyt and the city signed their 1997 agreement, slightly more than 30 percent of the two thousand units developed by Hoyt were affordable. Compared with development in most US cities, that was an impressive achievement, yet it fell short of the 35 percent requirement the company had agreed to. By 2014, Hoyt's affordable proportion was heading still lower, to 28 percent.[13] As a consequence, Hoyt, under its agreement with the city, was required to sell the city a quarter-block of land, at a discount. The city then arranged for a nonprofit developer to construct apartments on that parcel for low- to moderate-income people.[14]

By the most reliable recent estimate available, roughly a fifth of the Pearl's housing consisted of units inexpensive enough for below-average-income households to afford them. That figure was as of 2011.[15] Since then, the difficulties faced by people in the middle—households not

---

Ed McNamara, Maestro of Affordable Housing

Nobody has built more apartments in the Pearl for people of modest means than Ed McNamara, operator of Turtle Island Development. "I wanted to see community development done right—in a businesslike way, but with a social mission," said McNamara, who, in a career of more than forty years, has been a building contractor, director of a nonprofit community development corporation called REACH, and, for a time, advisor to Mayor Charlie Hales.

McNamara had noticed that good housing work by nonprofit groups tends not to get the attention it deserves. Consequently, in 2002, seven years after completing a Loeb Fellowship at Harvard's Graduate School of Design, he founded his for-profit development firm, specializing in affordable housing. "I thought," he said, "if a for-profit did the same stuff, nobody could ignore it."

In 2005, he was part of the team that built Sitka Apartments, a 210-unit, two-building complex for "workforce" residents, including families with children, on a block of the Pearl District bounded by NW Northrup and Overton Streets and NW Eleventh and Twelfth Avenues. Subsidized from a variety of sources, the six-story Sitka buildings included a higher proportion of two-bedroom apartments than other buildings in the Pearl had offered. It also offered a community room, a landscaped courtyard, laundry and recycling facilities, free Internet connections, and, just outside its doors, a stop for the Portland Streetcar. Turtle Island constructed the stop—by building a curb extension and a streetcar platform—so that residents would have convenient, inexpensive access to much of the city's core.[a]

Hardly anyone expected that families with children would choose to live in six-story buildings in the Pearl. McNamara's view, though, was that "family housing was needed to make this feel like a neighborhood." So, he

---

[a] Andy Giegerich, "Affordable Pearl Isn't a Fake," *Portland Business Journal*, June 13, 2004, http://www.bizjournals.com/portland/stories/2004/06/14/story1.html.

ngly did without the gates. Residents "kind of police their own
gs," Sweitzer said. The open midblock passages provided appeal-
rtcuts for pedestrians. For the most part, nonresidents "don't lin-
e long," Sweitzer said. "They know it belongs to the residents."
he city's homeless population became more conspicuous in the
gates were installed in a few locations. Whether they will become
n remains to be seen.

evelopment moved farther north, there was less context to relate
many of the new buildings adopted more contemporary styl-
th simple, straightforward shapes, smooth walls, and little or no
ornament, many of them did not feel as rich or idiosyncratic
best of the old buildings, but they made a decent backdrop to
eets. Balconies decorated by the residents provided evidence of
habitation, always an enlivening factor.

world economic crisis of 2008 and the sharp recession curtailed
evelopment in the Pearl for a few years, and some residents assert
e drop in construction led officials to lower the design standards.
really poor design has been approved in the North Pearl, postre-
," said Kate Washington, who chaired the Neighborhood Asso-
s Planning Committee. "The city was hungry for just anything
uilt. You can really feel the difference between the old neighbor-
hat has context versus the area to the north."

absence of retail in the ground floor of some recent North Pearl
gs has detracted from street life, said Stephenson, who directs
ironmental studies and sustainable urbanism program at Rollins
e in Winter Park, Florida, and who for years has owned a condo
Pearl. The underlying problem is that pedestrian traffic is much
in the North Pearl than farther south, and it frequently takes
while for new storefront space to attract tenants.

tail is hard," said Allan Classen, editor and publisher of *NW*
ner, a newspaper that covers Northwest Portland. Some spaces

poor enough to qualify for subsidies and not affluent enough to easily afford new urban housing—have grown. The affordability problem
exists not just in the Pearl but in the entire core of Portland and in some
of the neighborhoods beyond.

Portland's housing squeeze, which includes a persistent homelessness problem, has prompted a series of municipal responses. The city
council declared a "housing state of emergency" in October 2015 and

---

tailored his next project, the 138-unit Ramona, even more strongly to families and children, collaborating with the Portland school system to include
nearly 13,000 square feet of educational space on the building's ground
floor. Completed in 2011, the Ramona demonstrated that kids—some of
them in one-parent, others in two-parent families—would do well in such
a setting. The six-story Ramona became home, he reports, to more kids—
about 130 of them—than any other block in Portland.[b]

He found economies that help make the building affordable for low-
income families. "Three-bedroom, two-bath units are as small as 1,077
square feet," he said. "There's no air conditioning. There's no washer/dryer
in the unit." Offsetting those economies are such features as a community
room "where they can do kids' birthday parties, movie nights, storytelling
nights," he said.

"I keep my rents well below the maximum I can charge," he adds. "With
that, I can get much less vacancy, less turnover. My staff can spend time
with the tenants rather than showing units. The staff knows everything that
goes on in the building. Everybody gets a bonus, including the housekeeper.
I have virtually no turnover of the staff. It becomes a better place to live.
We upgrade constantly. When things wear out, we put in better stuff than
we had originally—better carpet, et cetera. The buildings pretty much look
like new."

Over the years, McNamara has developed more than one thousand units
of housing, but has now stopped doing affordable housing in Portland. "It's
too hard to do so as a for-profit developer," he explained. "I wouldn't do any
market-rate there because it would have to be upper-end rents, and I'm not
interested in doing that." Still, his buildings testify to what the Pearl, in its
best years, was able to accomplish.

[b] Craig Beebe, "Exploring Affordable Housing in NW Portland," 1000 Friends of
Oregon, June 26, 2012, https://www.friends.org/affordablehousingtour.

soon afterward allocated more than $100 million to deal with it. In March 2016, the state legislature, acting on a proposal supported by Portlanders, ended Oregon's ban on "inclusionary housing" ordinances. These ordinances, which require developers to make some of their new units affordable for low- to moderate-income residents, have long been adopted by local governments in some other states, most notably Montgomery County, Maryland. With the change in Oregon's law, Portland will be able to require developers to reserve up to 20 percent of the units in new projects for people who earn no more than 80 percent of the median income. In return, developers would get density bonuses or property tax exemptions.[16]

In November 2016, Portland voters approved a $258 million bond measure to create more housing for people of modest means. Among its aims is providing six hundred units for people who earn less than 30 percent of the median family income—roughly $22,000 for a family of four. The bond will be paid for by a property tax increase that will cost the average city homeowner about $75 a year.[17]

The city also recently increased the amount of tax-increment financing revenue it will spend on affordable housing. The raise—from 30 percent to 40 to 45 percent—could result in additional affordable housing in the urban renewal area. "It's hard to predict," McNamara acknowledged, "but I think the Pearl will continue to have a higher percentage of affordable housing than other neighborhoods."

The Struggle over Style

In deciding what kind of style their new buildings should have, developers and architects at first demonstrated a keen appreciation of context. New buildings took cues from old buildings nearby. In 1993, when Prendergast set out to test the market for new residential condominiums in the rail yards, he erected a three-story red-brick building, Pearl Lofts, with its entrance in a round brick arch. "Pearl Lofts blends in with the

early twentieth-century warehouses and oth
Pearl District," the Urban Land Institute sa

Many new structures were clad in red br
Their windows had predominantly vertical
of the old buildings. When Powell's City of
building at NW Eleventh Avenue and Co
building, the new construction was made to
ings. Included in the design were a decorativ
to adorn the walls and a corbelled parapet to
helped endow the building with visual detai

The Gregory Lofts, a twelve-story mix
pleted in 2000, took a somewhat different
1930s Art Deco, such as curving corners,
precedent in the Pearl. The Art Deco motif
however, and the Gregory had industrial sas
the old warehouses nearby, so the building

Buildings constructed in the Pearl in the
years of the twenty-first century mostly re
Pearl District," said Michael Mehaffy, a Por
ment consultant. They had, he said, "a comp
scale and detailing at pedestrian level."

The buildings maximized light and co
First-floor units in Pearl Lofts featured expa
dated by ceilings 12 feet high. "In a city that
winter days, people crave natural light," the
in its report on the building.

Many buildings were designed around sh
of which the occupants could relax in. Th
light into the apartments and generated a sen
developers thought that passages leading in
need locked gates for security, but as years

have remained empty for a year or more and then have been filled by high-end national retailers or by banks, a use that is visually humdrum. One alternative that has been tried is putting apartments or live/work units into some ground-floor spaces and designing them so that they can be converted to stores and cafes when traffic picks up.

Pedestrian traffic might multiply if the city would create a popular destination on the Willamette waterfront, Stephenson believes. So far, officials have not been willing to spend the money to do that.

Architects on the Neighborhood Association's planning committee, Classen notes, have repeatedly said, "We want some bolder architecture." They have called for "big buildings, bold buildings, tall buildings, hyperdensity." After the development hiatus brought on by the global financial crisis, some people were elated in 2013 when Hoyt moved forward with the Cosmopolitan, a twenty-eight-story reflective glass condo tower in the North Pearl. At 340 feet, the Cosmopolitan is the tallest building in Portland. Stephenson detests it.

"It sticks out; it doesn't fit in," he said. "The glare from it is such a blinding light." The Cosmopolitan stands between two parks, along a corridor that should be key to tying together different parts of the Pearl, yet according to Stephenson, "it eviscerates the view you want to have. It destroys any sense of visual continuity."[19]

In 2015, a high-rise called The NV was being built a few blocks from the Cosmopolitan. The NV's tower, rising from a full-block podium, was rotated 45 degrees from the city street grid. Rotating the tower maximized the inhabitants' views of the Willamette, but it detracted from the regularity and coherence of the Pearl's urban form.[20]

Mehaffy wrote a biting commentary in *Planetizen* about buildings that had been approved since about 2011, saying that "instead of clear, predictable form-based codes that guide development to blend sensitively with the scale of its neighbors and mitigate its impacts, the city imposes a subjective game of 'impress the design panelists' and

Seen in the foreground is part of the five-block Brewery Blocks complex developed by Gerding Edlen. The seven-building complex mixes old and new buildings as well as multiple uses, including stores, offices, housing, restaurants, and cultural attractions. (Photo courtesy of Gerding Edlen)

'who's the best renderer'—for drawings that are famously unlike the built result."[21]

Mehaffy argued that such buildings were symptomatic of a problem in architectural culture as a whole. "Architecture has become a novelty machine, in which the name of the game is to be exciting and dramatic and different—or at any rate like the latest fashion, which is different from the previous fashion, whatever that is," he said. "But this is not a problem-solving approach; it's a novelty-for-novelty's-sake approach."

It is hard to make a cohesive neighborhood out of buildings questing for novelty. "Urban residents have a basic need to make sense of their environments, and to find meaning and value in them," Mehaffy has insisted.[22]

At this point, the number of discordant buildings in the Pearl is still small. Most residents seem happy with the district overall. Not only does it have interesting, human-scale traditional buildings; it also has many Modern buildings that provide a satisfactory backdrop to the public realm. In the Brewery Blocks, one of the most outstanding developments in the district, new Modern structures and decades-old brick buildings make a dynamic combination.

Not all things contemporary are out of place, but the city needs to be skeptical about making architectural "boldness" the Pearl's calling card. The new and striking may achieve their aesthetic effect at the expense of more lasting qualities—qualities that make for a walkable environment.

Triumph of a "Pro-Urban Outlook"

Rick Gustafson, the former head of Portland's three-county metropolitan government and of the Portland Streetcar, traces the enormous progress of Portland back to 1973, when Neil Goldschmidt was elected mayor and ushered in changes in how officialdom dealt with planning, development, transportation, and the shaping of the region. What emerged "was an investment strategy essentially based on Jane Jacobs," Gustafson said. "It was outrageously controversial." Opponents—people who accepted the idea of a highway- and car-oriented metropolis—"really believed you were from the Moon," he said.

Controversy notwithstanding, over the years there remained "a stable support base of about 60 percent for planning." The pro-urban outlook was never dislodged from power. The constancy of support for a compact, pedestrian-oriented urban vision accounts, Gustafson said, for the scope of Portland's achievement, which is unrivaled among cities of its size.

The City of Portland set up an Office of Neighborhood Involvement to help neighborhoods work collaboratively with officials and bureaus; residents can exert influence through their neighborhood associations. The planning committee of the Pearl District Neighborhood Association, for instance, has the authority to examine land use, design, and

Cyclists pedaling from one of the Pearl District's chief grocery stores. Portland's network of neighborhood greenways for biking runs through the Pearl. (Photo by Philip Langdon)

transportation issues in the Pearl and tell the city bureaus what it would like to see done.

What does the Pearl need now? Certainly the neighborhood would be better if it had a full-fledged public elementary school or two. It could use a public library. Additional family-sized apartments would allow the Pearl to become a neighborhood with more children. There are a lot of births in the Pearl, and more young families might stay if they could obtain housing that meets their needs.

The Pearl is impressive because it does many things well, things that reinforce one another. The Pearl shows how to create relatively dense collections of apartments and townhouses, organized on the ground so that they make for good urban living. It shows how old buildings can be put to imaginative new uses and can accommodate creative sectors of the economy. The district embraces art, including public art. It has pioneered the rebirth of the streetcar system; since 2001, when the Portland Streetcar's first line began operating, many other cities have been inspired by Portland's example to build streetcar lines of their own. The Pearl places most necessities of daily life within walking distance; in many instances, those that are not within walking distance are just a quick streetcar ride away.

This 120-block area is a testament to what intelligent and energetic people, working together, can accomplish in a little more than thirty years (using the AIA's 1983 study as a starting point). Most of the district's achievements began to arrive in force only after the mid-1990s. Tremendous progress has been squeezed into two decades or less. If the district once consisted of a few pearls hidden behind rough shells, today the pearls abound. The buildings, streets, parks, and gathering places come together to form a great neighborhood. Building communities is demanding work, and Portlanders have plenty to show for it.

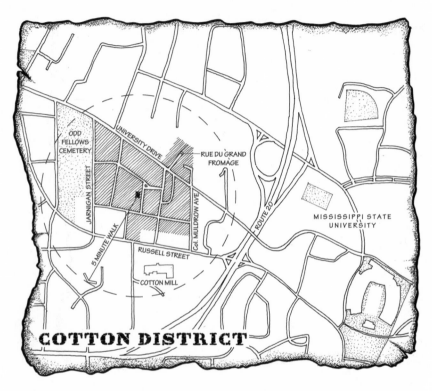

COTTON DISTRICT

Map of the Cotton District (shaded) and some of the surrounding area. Since Starkville adopted a form-based code in 2013, developers have built on Dan Camp's achievements by announcing new residential or mixed-use projects on University Drive and Russell Street, the district's northern and southern edges. (Drawing by Dhiru A. Thadani)

CHAPTER 6

Patient Placemaking: The Cotton District, Starkville, Mississippi

In 1995, when I was news editor at *Progressive Architecture*, the magazine published "The Placemaker," a story about a determined man who had spent most of his adult life building up a neighborhood in Starkville, Mississippi, that he called the Cotton District. Marilyn Avery, the article's author, observed that the Cotton District "appears to be a historic neighborhood with its combination of traditional architecture and finely grained urbanism—the kind of neighborhood where wealthy families tend to reside over many generations." She pointed out, however, that the district's buildings were in fact largely "designed and built by one person: Dan Camp, a former shop teacher with a personal interest in architecture and urban design."[1]

Photos of Camp's buildings, which seemed wholly in sympathy with handsome old buildings seen across the South, greatly impressed me, and a year later I was likewise impressed by Camp himself when I heard him speak in Charleston, South Carolina, at a gathering of the Congress for New Urbanism. The shop teacher turned developer—his full name,

Dan Camp on the Rue du Grand Fromage, which is spanned by the romantic, whimsical Cinderella house. The little three-story building charmingly terminates the view down a narrow brick street. (Photo by Philip Langdon)

In the Cotton District, not everything is lined up at right angles. Camp twists some of the streets and places buildings up against the curb for an organic feeling reminiscent of historic villages. (Photo by Philip Langdon)

rarely used, is Robert Daniel Camp—was independent minded, alternately fiery and humorous, and a fervent advocate for walkable communities filled with traditional architecture.

Nearly twenty years went by before I had an opportunity to visit the Cotton District, but when I finally got to eastern Mississippi, I was not disappointed. Camp's creations were essentially as Avery had reported: "Each door, window, fence, and gate is elegantly crafted with wood detailing evocative of buildings found in Savannah, Alexandria, and Charleston. . . . Pedestrian walkways connect an assortment of public and semipublic spaces and lead to narrow streets. Residents walk slowly and talk to each other on the street."

The roughly ten-block district contains slightly more than one hundred buildings owned by Camp and his family: 350 apartments, plus commercial spaces containing restaurants, bars, and other businesses. They are all the product of his many years of patient placemaking. Interspersed among Camp's properties are buildings belonging to other landlords, developers, and institutions. Their buildings are, for the most part, so ordinary as to be nearly unnoticeable; it is Camp's buildings that catch the eye and set the tone for the district. Variety abounds. His creations range from cottages as small as 12 by 22 feet to three-story mixed-use structures; all his buildings are in "traditional" styles, but in assorted shapes and borrowing from different places and periods. The Cotton District does not feel like it was produced by one person or one organization; rather, it feels like a neighborhood that has evolved over decades, incorporating divergent influences. Against the low initial expectations of the powers that be, the Cotton District has become the pride of Starkville, the liveliest address in this town of 23,000.

Camp came to construction and real estate development largely on his own. Born in 1941 in Baton Rouge, Louisiana, he was brought up in Tupelo, Mississippi, where his mother taught school. Elvis Presley was one of Mrs. Camp's sixth-grade pupils; a plaque at Elvis's birthplace says that she invited him to sing in front of the class and encouraged him with his guitar, which some considered a "hick" instrument, an accompaniment for hillbilly music.

At an early age, Dan received a copy of *The Boy Mechanic*. For a youngster who liked knowing how things were put together, that book, a perennial favorite from *Popular Mechanics*, was inspirational; it influenced the direction of his life. "When I was thirteen, I designed a cabin cruiser," Camp recalled, "and I learned proportions from that. I built that boat in the next three to four years with basically hand tools. I had no help. My family was not interested in those things."

University Drive at its juncture with Maxwell Street is the restaurant and nightlife hub of the Cotton District, with three-story buildings that have eating and drinking establishments on the ground floor and apartments above. Activity spills out of BIN 612 to enliven the intersection. (Photo by Jeremy Murdock, courtesy of The Cotton District)

He taught industrial arts briefly in Vicksburg and settled in Starkville in 1967 to teach blueprint reading, drafting, and shop classes at his alma mater, Mississippi State University. His wife wanted a house, and Camp resolved to build it himself. "So then," he said, "I got interested in real estate." In 1969, using winnings he had made in the stock market, he designed and constructed a two-story clapboard building containing eight rental apartments on Lummus Drive in a run-down neighborhood once called Needmore, near a defunct cotton mill. "Most folks, when asked about this location, thought it unwise," he said.[2] The neighborhood—it would be years before he dubbed it the Cotton District—consisted mainly of millworker housing of one-room-wide, several-room-deep dwellings on 25-by-100-foot lots. In the 1960s, he said, "most of the tenant housing was in a state of despair."

By the zoning standards of the time, the majority of the neighbor-hood's lots were substandard, but Camp was rebuilding a blighted dis-trict bit by bit, with money he raised himself, so officials were willing to grant him variances and let him build on lots that technically were too small. He tucked parking in where it would fit, sometimes at the rear of the properties. Many of the building plans he submitted to City Hall were little more than sketches on napkins. "The aldermen had no prob-lem," he said. "They said, 'Just don't go elsewhere in the city.'"

Displacement was not an issue. The cotton mill had closed in 1955, reopened under different ownership, and then closed for good in 1962. Most families of working age had already moved on by 1968, when Camp began his land purchases. Longtime Starkville alderman Mary Lee Beal, who rented one of Camp's first apartments in 1970, said the neighborhood's residents at that time were cotton mill retirees. "As they passed away, Dan and others purchased the property to turn into rentals."

The biggest thing in favor of the area Camp selected was geogra-phy: the neighborhood was about a ten-minute walk from the univer-sity's western edge. Downtown Starkville was about a twenty-minute walk in the other direction, down University Drive. Camp had found Starkville's urbanistic sweet spot.

By 1972, he had built a total of sixteen rental units and was netting more income from the apartments than from his teaching job, so he quit the university and became a full-time independent contractor. He built houses for himself, for clients, and on spec in or near Starkville. In the Cotton District itself, he created apartments that he filled pri-marily with students. He charged market rates; today, his monthly rents range from $1.25 to $1.75 a square foot. The rents are, and were, not cheap, but because of the units' small size, they were afford-able. A single person might rent a freestanding cottage measuring just 16 by 20 feet (plus sleeping loft). Tenants, including a smattering of

This approximately 14-by-28-foot cottage on Cotton Row has a presence out of proportion to its size, thanks to its Classical form. The front porch helps compensate for the interior's limited square footage. (Photo by Philip Langdon)

academics and professionals, liked Camp's units because of their tall ceilings, porches, balconies, landscaped outdoor spaces, and unusually fine construction.

How to Build It

As Avery observed: "Camp's approach to the development of the Cotton District has been intuitive and personal. He loves woodworking and building. He admires traditional architecture and has spent countless hours studying and sketching traditional architecture in historic neighborhoods in Vicksburg, Savannah, New Orleans, Alexandria, Natchez, and small Southern towns."[3] He has amassed a library of reference books, such as the authoritative eight-volume *New Orleans Architecture* series. He also has taken his travels further afield, bringing back ideas from historic buildings in Italy, Belgium, Great Britain, and elsewhere.

It is one thing to admire traditional architecture and quite another to build it, especially when the cost has to be competitive with conventional development. Camp's solution to these challenges was to train his own workers to make columns, capitals, doors, windows, and shutters, all properly proportioned in traditional styles. He set up a woodworking shop behind his own four-story Charleston side-yard home that he erected in the heart of the Cotton District. There Camp's employees turn out building components that meet his exacting standards.

"Window sash," Camp said, "is made the old-fashioned way," with mortise and tenon durably holding the mullions in place. Stair treads are made with a bullnose edge and a cove underneath. Shutters have mortise-and-tenon construction.

The workshop foreman, a quiet man named Abraham Lincoln Prater Jr., started working for Camp before he was out of high school and has been with him since the 1970s. Of Prater, Camp said: "He can take a broken twelve-light window and reconstruct it in our shop."

Camp has modified his use of employee-craftsmen over the years. The crew has stopped making doors for the most part; Camp now buys them from an outside source, although, he noted, "we still have the knowledge base to do a door if a student kicks in a door." He stopped

Dan Camp (center), developer of the Cotton District, explains a construction detail to employee J. D. Jones as another construction employee, Eric Rice, looks on. At rear is the shop in which many components of Camp's buildings are made. (Photo by Philip Langdon)

making wooden windowsills and lintels because they became a maintenance headache, especially on the buildings' south faces that are exposed to Mississippi heat and rain. Instead, the crew makes sills and lintels of custom-formed cement. The crew also uses handmade wooden molds to make the cement stair treads.

He also quit making millwork in-house, partly to speed production and partly because it became too humdrum. "He does things until the challenge becomes old hat," said Neil Strickland, a member of Camp's office staff from 2013 to 2016. "He's all about new challenges—trying new challenges just to see if he can do them. It promotes pride in workmanship."

One Cotton District apartment features a freestanding spiral staircase. "We steamed the oak to bend it," Camp said. On a tour of the district, he points to "a $10,000 Palladio curved window that takes up the whole second floor of a cottage." For that window, he said, the crew had the painstaking task of replicating Palladian details correctly. He gestures toward a large and refined dormer that the crew built at ground level and then hoisted—complete—into position on the slope of a roof. That unusual method enabled the crew to achieve higher-quality craftsmanship than would have been possible otherwise. A sophisticated dormer "is like a piece of furniture," he said. "It's a challenge—like building a boat as a thirteen-year-old kid."

Most American residential buildings have gutters that hang from the eaves. In the Cotton District, by contrast, some buildings have gutters incorporated into the cornice, which are more pleasing to look at than conventional exposed gutters.

"On a house we started thirty years ago, we made all the doors and transoms of two-thousand-year-old cypress," Camp said. By his account, cypress logs 4 to 5 feet in diameter had fallen into Moon Lake in the Mississippi Delta in the 1920s; when they were rediscovered during a drought decades later, Camp was able to obtain the logs, mill the fine-grained wood—"they smelled like apple cider"—and make building components that resist rotting.

Camp disdains plastic. Countertops are made of cement, which the workers pour from a cone. The counters' profiles are shaped with a mold made by the workers themselves. "We get that cast stone look," he explained. Many buildings have exteriors of stucco, chosen in part for its appearance. On a group of duplexes known as the Mississippi Houses, the stucco has been slightly rusticated to resemble stone blocks. (Having one material imitate another, more costly material is a long-accepted practice in traditional architecture, although there are limits beyond which it is frowned upon.)

On a row of townhouses, the stucco was initially a dark purple, but over the years, it has faded unevenly. Camp does not seem especially bothered; he likes patina. "We don't want anything to be too perfect," he said. For walkways, he buys number 2 bricks, those with small flaws. "We work very hard not to have the Disney look." On the other hand, he does avoid shortcuts that would disrupt the intended aesthetic effect. When moisture penetrated some stucco walls and caused framing members or wallboard to rot, he took pains to get at the decay from the interior of the building, leaving the exterior stucco surface uncut.

Little Homes with Character

With his incremental mode of development, Camp buys properties when they are put up for sale and figures out how to make the most of them. Sometimes, an existing building can be renovated and rented out. Years later, he might return, tear down the renovated building, and build something larger, more remunerative, or more elegantly styled. His methods add to the district's richness of character and make the surroundings more interesting for walking.

Some of his tiny residences are mundane, but many others possess stateliness. He has a fondness for small dwellings that look like they stepped out of the Greek Revival era. A few have rooflines with statues attached. The statuary "is a whimsical thing I did when I had a trip to Italy," he said. He's not putting up statuary anymore. "My wife put a stop to it."

When Camp acquires enough land, he builds a larger group of apartments. The question then becomes how to give the assemblage of apartments an aura of dignity. Often, he builds what looks like a two- or three-story, classically styled single-family house but divides the interior into small rental units. The apartments sit inside a building that has symmetrically composed windows, a traditional pitched roof, and a domestic-scale center entrance.

Modernism promulgated the idea that a building can be designed "from the inside out," letting the needs of the interior determine the nature of the exterior. For architects, this concept was liberating, but it frequently had the unintentional result of harming the public realm. It is not uncommon for a Modern building to present an awkward or antisocial face—even a blank wall—to the street and to passersby.

Camp's method is almost the reverse. He prizes a symmetrical or balanced exterior, and when symmetry conflicts with internal needs, the internal arrangements may have to yield. "Windows are there for proportion," he said. When he was designing a particularly prominent building—a three-story, mixed-use structure on University Drive— Camp discovered that if he gave the facade a succession of evenly spaced windows (crucial to the building's sense of decorum), it was going to be nearly impossible to fit closets into some of the rooms. He toyed with placing certain windows in closets but scotched that idea. Ultimately, it became clear that the solution was for the crew to build armoires rather than closets for those rooms. As Camp sees it, each tenant ended up having a nice piece of furniture in which to store clothing, and the public realm ended up with a very good-looking building.

Cotton District buildings have been described as simultaneously dignified and homespun. Victor Dover, an architect in Coral Gables, Florida, said: "Despite the fact that so many parts are a little bit off—headers above windows seem short, proportions stretched and squashed, ornaments oversized or undersized, porches so shallow, and so on—the result is still charming."[4] How can you not admire a builder-developer who does things like mix marble dust into cast concrete steps to make them shine like stone?

"When he's got a project going," Strickland said, "he thinks about every aspect of the project, how to do it, how to make it more creative, more cost effective to maintain. He balances all those trade-offs, and that's why the buildings are wise beyond their years."

An apartment building on Lummus Street in the Cotton District gives the impression of being a substantial single-family house. Dan Camp produces groups of apartments that convey dignity and make a presentable streetscape. (Photo by Philip Langdon)

Indoors and Out

Over time, Camp has become a believer in providing as much natural light as possible and in maximizing connections to landscape and the outdoors. "We put in as many windows as we can," he said. "They're a minimum of 6 feet high. We slam 'em to the top plate with very little header. A tenant can put a couch under the window, and it won't impede the light."

He builds balconies and is especially proud of the continuous balconies on a building on Rue du Grand Fromage ("Street of the Big Cheese"). Curved at the ends, similar to those of old buildings in New Orleans, the balconies intensify the intimacy of the narrow brick street. He builds front porches, which make the streets more gregarious. He builds decks.

A sign attached to a building announces the "Street of the Big Cheese." (Drawing by Dhiru A. Thadani)

Of the many balconies, porches, and decks, Camp said, "Students use them, whereas adults tend to lock up everything they're doing."

Philip Bess, an architecture professor at the University of Notre Dame, periodically takes graduate students to Starkville to experience the Cotton District and learn about Camp's methods. Bess pointed out one of the curiosities of the development. Depicted on a map, "it doesn't look like much. There's no big centralized space. There's nothing monumental," he said. The geometry of the overall plan is loose and appears to be just a collection of narrow streets and somewhat irregular blocks. There was no master plan when the neighborhood was first built, and Camp has not imposed one since, but, Bess said, Camp has developed the area in ways that add value and enhance livability.

What is particularly creative, Bess said, is the strategy Camp has applied to the interiors of blocks. He has arranged buildings into mews, courts, and other groupings. He has created drives and walkways that are enjoyable whether you are in a car, on a bike, or on foot. The outdoor spaces and passages present gardens and yards of varying dimensions, but not overly large. "The smaller the space, the better," Camp said. Bess sees in Camp's shaping of the blocks' internal spaces

Entry path to a cottage. Throughout the Cotton District, passages and landscape elements are orchestrated to add pleasure to outdoor spaces and to movement. (Photo by Philip Langdon)

a familiarity with the blocks, courts, and passages of New Orleans' beguiling French Quarter.

The blocks have also been compared to those in colonial Philadelphia and Charleston. In those old cities, mansions were erected at the edges of the blocks, whereas cottages and outbuildings—including servants' quarters, kitchens, workshops, and stables—were built in the blocks' centers, forming diverse compounds that are human-scale and full of interesting detail.[5] Some Cotton District blocks achieve a density of twenty-eight units an acre, yet they possess plenty of privacy.

Off University Drive, the district's main thoroughfare, Camp built the cozy Rue du Grand Fromage, a brick street one lane wide that feels like an amalgam of French Quarter and Old Europe. The view down the street focuses on a fanciful building three stories high, topped by a cupola, known locally as the "Cinderella house." He threaded the street through a tight arch in the building's ground floor, knowing that the result would be a surprising and distinctive setting.

Across the neighborhood, buildings rarely form a precisely straight line along a street. Instead, they respond to the peculiarities of their sites so that, for example, trees do not have to be cut down. No single pavement, curb detail, or dimension is adhered to throughout. Brick patterns, street widths, terraced sidewalks, garden walls, and fences adjust to circumstance, giving the Cotton District an aura of authenticity.

Managing for the Long Haul

In the mid-1980s, near Russell Street on the neighborhood's southern edge, Camp built a brick street not much wider than an alley, lined on both sides by two-and-a-half-story rowhouses. He named it Planters Row and wrote covenants allowing commercial activity on the first floor of the rowhouses. Unlike everything else he had developed in the district, he sold the units, on 30-by-36-foot lots, to buyers with the idea that a street full of homeowners would help give the neighborhood permanence. It was a disappointment. The little commercial enterprises that he had anticipated on Planters Row never took root, perhaps because the location was out of the way or perhaps because the 9½-foot-wide street and its minuscule sidewalks were too cramped.

What most bothered Camp about Planters Row, though, was that he lost money on it. The project confirmed in him his original business practice: build and hold; do not sell. Since then, he has remained resolute that the most feasible way of developing a well-crafted, mixed-use neighborhood is to buy properties, design buildings for them, assign his own crew do much of the finish work (subcontractors are used for rough construction), rent them out, and manage them. That is how he and his sons, Robert and Bonn, have accumulated such a large stock of buildings.

Camp believes that investing time and money to generate customized buildings designs, make many of the building components, and tailor the landscape only makes sense if he retains ownership, collecting a steady stream of rent as the properties rise in value. In Starkville, at least, he does not believe that he can make money on such high-quality accommodations if he sells them upon completion, sacrificing long-term appreciation.

Consistent with his methods, he and his staff run an office that rents out the units and takes care of maintenance and repairs. Every morning, Camp gathers the construction and maintenance crew—usually eight to ten men—in the office at 7:00 and lays out duties for the day. They learn that an apartment is having a water leak again, after the ceiling had already been repaired. A heat pump has gone bad. The gas has been turned off in a unit. Some fool of a tenant went into an attic, where he had no business going, and fell through the ceiling below. A truck backed into a building and damaged a cornerboard. Trash, strewn about after a big college football game, must be cleaned up.

Camp, a furrowed brow on his worn face, long vertical wrinkles below his eyes, listens, leads, gives orders, and launches side excursions into news and politics. He tries to draw the men into discussing the issues of the day. When I was present, many of them seemed to hold back. Dan by his own admission is "ornery," and perhaps the employees would rather just do their jobs.

By 7:20 or so, the meeting breaks up. A few minutes later, an alderman and a former alderman take seats in the same comfortable front room and have a political discussion that the employees seemed reluctant to engage in. After that, it is time for Camp to get on the phone and argue with a utility company that has strained his patience. There is an unending sequence of matters to be resolved, repairs to be made, and tenants to be heard. Annie Higgins, Camp's long-serving business manager, sits at a desk nearby, calmly helping the Cotton District handle daily difficulties.

Offsetting the hassles are repeated satisfactions. People admire what Camp has accomplished. Jason Walker, an alderman and a landscape architecture professor, said the Cotton District has given Starkville a sense of place it previously did not have. "We don't have a square, we don't have a river. We have the Cotton District," Walker said. When the chamber of commerce promotes Starkville, he noted, "it will always have one photo of the Cotton District." When Mississippi State University wants to celebrate an athletic triumph, it often does so in the district, which is well supplied with restaurants and bars. The Cotton District "is very much the cultural center of the community," said Parker Wiseman, a former Camp tenant who has been mayor of Starkville since 2009.

Mary Lee Beal, a former alderman, said that the Cotton District "gave people a place to hang out. It is so different from the past. At 2:30 in the afternoon, there are students sitting in a casual, relaxed area." She added, "Years ago, there was no place to eat."

In tribute to his achievement, the people of Starkville elected Camp mayor in 2005. In office, he saw to it that a new police station and city courthouse were built in the downtown, not at a highway location. He hired a full-time planner to begin preparing a new comprehensive plan. Starkville was one of forty municipalities across the nation recognized by the US Environmental Protection Agency as "smart growth" cities. Starkville adopted Mississippi's first sustainability policy, promoting green development and requiring LEED certification for any public building in excess of 3,000 square feet.

After his term ended, the city adopted a transect-based zoning code, prepared by the consulting group PlaceMakers, that encourages compact, walkable development. The code, which authorizes dense, mixed-use development along many of the city's corridors, is credited with sparking recent multistory housing, some containing retail on the ground floor, on the edges of the Cotton District and on the periphery of downtown.[6]

Larry Box, the city's former school superintendent, pointed out that Camp previously served on the board of education and was a strong supporter of the city's public schools, which had lost most of their white students after a desegregation order. "Under the loud, gruff exterior, there's a tender heart," said Box. "He really cares about making a difference for people." That includes the construction and maintenance people. Strickland, Camp's former employee, observed that Camp knows "how to do and how to sequence every step of every task involved in the hourly cultivation and maintenance of the district" and described Camp's methods of working with employees:

> Any capability that Dan wants to have on the ground he has to first educate in his workmen. He keeps mental track of what each one can do, and daily designs in his head the neighborhood assignments of up to a dozen employees to best:
> - fit the skills they have relative to others,
> - keep them busy hour by hour,
> - take care of whatever comes up, and, sometimes,
> - develop the new skills he wants them to have.

Perhaps it's not so tough to optimize these four factors together, since his set of mentees is kept small and he is fully free to revise his morning plans throughout the day, after each new update from the work sites. Still, the attention he pays is impressive.

Most of Dan's workmen are people society never gives a chance, who walked onto his operation after dropping out of high school, getting out of prison, losing a loved one. His relationship with his workers is a flexible hybrid of business interest and fatherly friendship. The crew is not exactly welcome in the office outside of morning meeting and afternoon clock-out, but if anyone needs him for anything, they know they can come to him with their joys and troubles.

Encouraging Young Entrepreneurs

A walkable community has to have useful things for people to walk to. Camp has brought into the Cotton District an array of businesses, most of them small. The district lacks enough residents to support a full-line grocery store or a large clothing store, but it contains bars, restaurants, hair salons, a travel agency, a cigar lounge, a purveyor of smoked meats, and other enterprises.

"Dan has always been encouraging of entrepreneurs who have an idea and want to make it work," said Jessica Cheek, who, at age twenty-five, opened a juice and smoothie bar in 2014 in a tall-ceilinged 23-by-17-foot space next to the Rue du Grand Fromage. Barton Dinkins, who started Two Brothers Smoked Meats at age twenty-four in a 560-square-foot space, said he appreciated having a shop small enough to allow him to operate "with very minimal overhead and not get overwhelmed."

"These spaces were designed for young people who sat around their dorm rooms talking about things they'd like to do," Camp said, He sets the beginning rents low. "I start them off at $300 a month. Some are now $600 a month."

A member of the maintenance crew touches up a building on the Rue du Grand Fromage. Camp's business philosophy calls for retaining ownership of the buildings he develops. He employs a staff to manage and maintain the properties. (Photo by Philip Langdon)

He coaches the budding entrepreneurs and their employees, advising them on products or services they could provide and how to interact with customers. If he sees someone using a poor technique, he is not shy about pointing it out. The Camps "made me feel like I was part of the community," said Caleb Nabors, chef at a restaurant called Commodore Bob's, adding, "He expects a certain level of improvement/impressiveness."

If an operator works hard, success usually follows. Dinkins said word of mouth is enough to introduce a new shop in the Cotton District. "Because the community is so tight-knit, word can travel pretty fast," he said. "I didn't do any advertising."

A Leaner Urbanism

"This was a shoestring type of urban development," Camp said. It has made him wealthy, though, and it has improved life for people in Starkville. The question is, can the methods Camp employed in the Cotton District be applied in other cities and towns?

They can, but Camp had an unusual collection of advantages. First, property prices in the neighborhood were extremely low for many years. Second, Camp had practical skills. He understood construction and could teach others the hands-on techniques that he himself had mastered. Third, although Camp was not professionally trained in architecture, he had a good eye for design. Fourth, municipal regulation was minimal for much of his career as a developer.[7]

In Camp's view, developers in the United States do not know how to limit their costs. "The problem is that everybody depends on planners, engineers, architects, and by the time they get all these professionals involved, they can't afford the project," he said. "That's pretty well the case across the country." Together, those factors hinder the kind of development he believes in: human-scale, well-crafted places that get better as more is added to them over the years.

The pair of mild-yellow buildings at the entrance to the Rue du Grand Fromage contain first-floor commercial space and upper-floor apartments. The short street, with parking spaces discreetly tucked away, features several shops small enough that first-time business operators can afford them. (Photo by Philip Langdon)

Close observers of New Urbanism, such as Notre Dame's Philip Bess, nonetheless see the Cotton District as a development that many can learn from. "I think it is a great model," Bess said. "Compare the stuff he's built to what 95 percent of developers build."

One thing a young developer following in Camp's footsteps might do to increase the chance of success is to focus at least partly on rental housing. New Urbanist developers have tended to build and sell rather than build, rent out units, and manage and maintain them. Camp is adamant that maintaining ownership of properties is what enables a developer to weather the economic ups and downs of the housing market. A potential pitfall is that a largely rental community will not have as many people who stay for decades. In the long run, most neighborhoods benefit from having homeowners—families and individuals who have a financial stake in the neighborhood—but rental units are still greatly needed, especially near universities.

The story of Dan Camp illustrates the crucial role that small developers play. "Legendary places like Greenwich Village were developed by small actors, not large actors," Strickland pointed out. "You can't just rely on real estate investment trusts. They're too risk-averse. It's the small guys who are oblivious enough to risk. That's what 'Lean Urbanism' is about. How do we keep things tenable for these guys?"

New Urbanists came up with the concept of Lean Urbanism in 2013, and a year later it was formally launched, as the Project for Lean Urbanism, under the auspices of the Center for Applied Transect Studies.[8] The focus of Lean Urbanism is on devising and promoting techniques that make it feasible for development to occur in small increments, such as one or two or just a few lots at a time rather than entire blocks or huge tracts.

Miami architect Andres Duany, a leading proponent of Lean Urbanism, asserts that in many locales in recent decades, too many rules and requirements have stifled independent action and made it difficult to carry out economical, small-scale development.[9] The prevailing system gets in the way of individuals who might accomplish, in their own communities, what Dan Camp has accomplished in Starkville.

"Infrastructure has become so gold-plated and expensive," Duany said. He pointed to present-day electrical codes that make it impossible to renovate an old apartment building without ripping out the old wiring and installing a new system at great expense. "Now, they will say the rules are necessary to protect health and safety. But we're going to do the empirical studies to show that's not the case," he said. "Most of us are living with the old electrical code, and we're just fine."[10]

Small-scale development has also been hampered by the tendency of municipal governments and economic development agencies to seek big projects orchestrated by developers (often from out of town or out of state) who have access to tens of millions or hundreds of millions of dollars. Developers with deep pockets are often the only ones who can tolerate cumbersome, slow-moving government processes, yet projects built by big developers have frequently failed to deliver the variety and human scale that a local person like Camp brings to a neighborhood. "I've come to think," said Philip Bess, "that great places are not made by outsiders."

Lean Urbanists want to foster independent, local developers and generate more small projects that bolster a sense of place. Doing so requires a rethinking of current rules and procedures.

Across the country, there are many individuals who aspire to build better communities. Some of them have settled in small cities, where regulatory barriers are often less daunting than in large metropolises. In small cities, costs are also frequently lower. If the Lean Urbanists are correct, some version of the path taken by Dan Camp may be the route to creating a new generation of distinctive, walkable neighborhoods.

Camp has a refrain he recites when he feels like a voice crying in the wilderness: "Nobody knows how to do what we do." It is important that people know about Camp. It is important to know how a rundown old neighborhood in Starkville, in one of the poorest states in the nation, became a marvelous place.

Conclusion: Toward Human-Scale Communities

In the previous chapters, we looked at six walkable communities and at what makes them satisfying places to live. Those examples might help you see ways to improve your own community. From my own experience and from observing neighborhoods, towns, and cities around the country, I have become convinced that places organized at the pedestrian scale are, on balance, the healthiest and most rewarding places to live and work.

In recent decades, neighborhoods in many older cities and towns have become increasingly livable, in part because groups of people resolved to do something good in or for their community. In Center City Philadelphia, the revival owes much to the intimate character that many neighborhoods had all along. Narrow, slow-traffic streets with slender rowhouses bumping up against the sidewalks helped residents get to know one another, which in turn helped them work together for the common good. Hangouts such as cafes, corner taverns, parks, and squares, even when they were tattered after years of deterioration, gave people places to gather and rally. As time went by, neighborhood spirit blossomed, ushering in the current reality of reduced crime, new shops and amenities, and more and better housing.

On East Passyunk Avenue in Philadelphia, public seating gives the elderly, and people of every age, opportunities to rest. Anyone who walks also needs to sit down at times. The mural in the background, by Jared Vader, is called "Pathology of Devotion." (Photo by Philip Langdon)

In many places across the United States, community improvement got a crucial boost from local culture, from the set of customs and attitudes that becomes ingrained in a place over time. Local culture is certainly part of the story in Portland, Oregon. Portland was not a city of much note until the early 1970s, when it began its course of continuous improvement, but there was something in its history that was auspicious. Carl Abbott, a professor of urban studies and planning at Portland State University, points to Portland's history as a "moralistic community," one in which people have long focused—more than is the case in individualistic cultures—on pursuing the public good. New Englanders who guided Oregon's Willamette Valley settlements in their formative years planted this moralistic tendency, and it has remained a recurrent feature of the region, memorably manifested in Governor Tom McCall's 1973 warning against "sagebrush subdivisions, coastal condomania, and the ravenous rampages of suburbia." When this moralism had an upsurge in the 1960s and 1970s, one of the results was the establishment of a statewide planning system that aimed to make Oregon, in McCall's phrase, "the environmental model for the nation."[1]

Brattleboro, Vermont, bears some spiritual resemblance to Portland. The culture of Brattleboro displayed a noticeable social consciousness as far back as the nineteenth century. "Hospitality to strangers and interest in their diversity" was encouraged by "water-cure" operations like the Brattleboro Hydropathic Establishment, which used water from a local spring to relieve visitors' ailments.[2] A receptiveness to strangers with differing outlooks, and a willingness to pursue personal and social ideals, became conspicuous again in the 1960s and 1970s, when communes formed in the area and organizations like the Brattleboro Food Co-op were founded.

Residents of Chicago's Little Village likewise had an encouraging culture they could draw from: a Mexican tradition of social protest that found expression in Cesar Chavez's organizing of farm laborers in the United States in the 1960s and 1970s. The Mexican practice of joining together to object to inequity helped inspire fifteen women in Little Village to launch a 2001 hunger strike that brought their community a sorely needed high school. The community's culture of protest and organization also helped bring about the new La Villita Park, community gardens, dozens of block clubs, and the West Thirty-First Street bus line. A powerful strain of civic activism was embedded in the local culture.

Community regeneration seems to progress in an organic fashion. People first join together for a purpose, such as obtaining healthier food. Their strivings, optimism, and a bit of success eventually lead them to focus on additional issues or challenges. In Brattleboro, the expanding agenda can be seen in discussions about whether the Co-op should build its new store in the center of town, where it will be accessible to people who do not have cars, and later in the question of whether to construct affordable apartments on top of the grocery store. Collective action, once it produces results, becomes a community habit; it becomes ingrained in the local character.

In *The Abundant Community*, John McKnight and Peter Block noted that small groups of people who get together because of a shared affinity are often the nucleus for community betterment. Their initial reason for associating with one another could be a taste for discussing fiction, a love of watching dogs play together, or any number of other activities. Through coming together to pursue a shared interest, people act on their enthusiasms, and the ground is thus prepared for community action. "Our communities are abundant with the resources we need for the future," McKnight and Block wrote. "It is the awakening of families and neighborhoods to these resources that is needed."[3]

How Neighborhoods Can Act
The capacity to build a richly satisfying, socially responsible community grows as it is nurtured. Steven Reed Johnson is a Portland community activist who has closely studied the dynamics of his city's

neighborhoods.[4] He discovered that since the early 1970s, Portland residents have become increasingly effective at civic improvement: "In effect, Portlanders have learned the rewards and problems of active citizenship through practice."[5] Once neighborhood groups take on a number of small challenges and achieve success, "then bureaucrats and officials notice," Johnson observed. Very early in Portland's renaissance, in 1974, the city established an Office of Neighborhood Involvement to help neighborhoods organize and collaborate with municipal government; the office now works with ninety-five neighborhood associations.

A less extensive system of collaboration between municipal government and neighborhood organizations has arisen in cities such as Philadelphia and New Haven. The City of Philadelphia officially recognizes "registered community organizations" (RCOs). The local RCO is notified by the planning commission when a zoning variance or special exception has been requested in its area or when a development requiring civic design review has been proposed. The RCO then convenes a public meeting, which the applicants must attend before zoning officials will hear the case. In New Haven, there are community management teams that hold neighborhood meetings; in East Rock, the meetings, once a month, give residents a chance to discuss their public safety concerns with the head of their police district and to have fruitful talks with developers about real estate projects being proposed. Neither the Philadelphia nor the New Haven program is as far-reaching as Portland's system, but they are informative and they often help neighborhoods to get some of the things they want.

Portland's Office of Neighborhood Involvement is probably less effective now than it was in its early years, but it is not the only innovation Portland has generated. For some time, the city offered transportation planning and land-use planning classes to members of the public as a way to help residents understand the systems they were trying to influence. "Civic skills," in Johnson's view, "are needed for citizens to be effective." Portland cultivated those skills, which raised the level of debate and facilitated public involvement. The classes educated thousands of people. Educational efforts of this sort—and in general, municipal encouragement of neighborhood-based activity—could benefit many towns and cities by giving citizens a larger voice in government. In McKnight and Block's words, "We, together, become the producers of a satisfying future."

One thing that has changed over the years is that neighborhood associations have to share the civic stage with many other citizen-based organizations. The proliferation of civic and advocacy groups has complicated the outlook for neighborhood associations, which now have to compete for volunteers and support against groups that focus on all sorts of individual concerns, from the environment to schools to racial disparities.

Johnson thinks that neighborhood associations need to avoid concentrating overwhelmingly on homeowner concerns, such as maintenance of property values; "homeowner values" can get in the way of looking out for the well-being of the entire community, which includes renters and people outside the neighborhood. Ideally, a neighborhood association should be willing to support action that serves the greater good, even if it goes against narrow self-interest.

Another influence on civic activism is that many people, especially millennials, have grown impatient with working through conventional channels. In an age of social media and instant, around-the-clock communication, there is a hunger for timely, direct action. This desire for swift responses helps account for the popularity of SeeClickFix, a web tool developed in New Haven that lets people electronically report nonemergency neighborhood issues to local government agencies.

Stepping Up the Pace

Neighborhoods need to come up with more spontaneous ways of working. Two examples of how that can be done are the City Repair Project in Portland and Tactical Urbanism, a community improvement strategy that emphasizes short-term, low-cost interventions and policies, which, it is hoped, will lead toward long-term results.

The City Repair Project started in 1996 in Sellwood, in southeast Portland, when Mark Lakeman and his neighbors decided to turn an ordinary intersection into a sociable, engaging community space. One weekend, they painted a large, flamboyant design on the street pavement. Officials in the Portland Bureau of Transportation were infuriated; they considered the streets to be the bureau's domain, not something the neighbors could alter at will. Around the intersection, Lakeman recounted, the group built various structures: "a bench, a lending library, a 24-hour tea stand, a children's playhouse, a kiosk for sharing neighborhood information," thus turning a transportation facility into "an interactive social space." They called the suddenly much more engaging intersection Share-It-Square. According to Lakeman, "At first, everybody was telling us that we had broken the law, but once they saw what we'd actually done, they wanted to figure out how to do it again."[6]

The street painting slowed traffic, increased neighborhood involvement, and may have reduced crime. Mayor Vera Katz liked the results, so city officials soon authorized this form of collective action throughout Portland. Some fifty other intersections have since been painted, and the City Repair Project has become a 501(c)3 nonprofit corporation, its budget paid for through donations and grants. "City Repair lets neighborhoods realize their inherent power to create places on their own," Alyse Nelson and Tim Shuck wrote in a study of the organization.[7] The volunteer City Repair organization educates people on why community space is important and teaches methods of consensus building. When the public participates in making decisions, people become less fearful of changes being advocated, and the results often win wider acceptance.

Tactical Urbanism, a grassroots movement in many communities across the United States, is similar: people dream up and carry out inexpensive interventions aimed at making public spaces more inviting and comfortable. "Megaprojects are not going to solve our problems, and we need to find a workaround to the challenge of building and retrofitting our cities," asserts Anthony Garcia of Miami, who teamed up with Mike Lydon in Brooklyn to run a firm called Street Plans Collaborative and then to promote Tactical Urbanism. In their view, "small, often short-term, easy to implement projects could have just as powerful an impact on the culture of a city as the megaprojects."[8] Garcia and Lydon help citizens work together; as local people get involved and public and private institutions and nonprofits join in, social capital grows.

Sometimes the actions taken are officially authorized and at other times not. Here are a few things that Tactical Urbanists have done:

- Painted crosswalks where they were missing or no longer visible.
- Conducted a "park-in" by temporarily parking cars along a curb where parking is normally prohibited, which slowed speeding traffic and showed that the roadway needed to be calmed to make the neighborhood more livable.
- Converted an on-street parking space, for one day, into a green landscape or a seating area.
- Temporarily painted bike lanes on streets to show citizens and public officials the possibilities.
- Temporarily installed landscaping on pavement to test whether the area could be converted into a public square.

Some Tactical Urbanism methods have been employed by municipal governments, nonprofits, and other organizations. For example, Janette Sadik-Khan, when she was New York City transportation commissioner, temporarily shut part of the street space in Times Square to vehicular traffic and put chairs on the pavement. When it became clear that people enjoyed sitting there and that vehicular traffic was not brought to

"Chair-bombing"—making seats from shipping pallets and putting them in public spaces that need them—is a tactic some people are using to make the urban environment more welcoming. This chair-making session took place during a Tactical Urbanism workshop organized in Boston by the New England Chapter of the Congress for New Urbanism. (Photo by Philip Langdon)

a standstill, the city took the next step: installing a permanent public plaza. On the other side of the country, Portland has allowed food trucks to cluster semipermanently along the edges of parking lots, creating inexpensive outdoor dining areas and enlivening areas that had been dull.

Some citizen interventions—for example, "chair-bombing" (making chairs from shipping pallets and placing them wherever public seating is needed, such as near bus stops)—may not qualify as Tactical Urbanism because they are not aimed at forcing long-term change. They nonetheless make the public environment more enjoyable, and they get people thinking about the need for public comfort.

Reforming Local Codes

Beyond Tactical Urbanism are many other actions governments can take to make a community more walkable, enjoyable, and affordable. Better zoning codes, such as the form-based codes that New Urbanists introduced, can upgrade the physical character of a developing or redeveloping area.

In 2013, encouraged by Dan Camp's accomplishments in the Cotton District, the City of Starkville, Mississippi, adopted a customized version of the SmartCode, a form-based code originally conceived by the Miami architecture and planning firm Duany Plater-Zyberk & Company. Within two years, developers began committing themselves to constructing dense, mixed-use projects on two corridors between downtown Starkville and Mississippi State University.

At the heart of the SmartCode is the idea that towns and cities should be structured as a series of walkable neighborhoods containing a mix of residential, office, and retail uses; that public spaces should generate more of a sense of enclosure; and that the transportation system should offer better and broader options for pedestrians. Starkville's code, produced by the consulting group PlaceMakers, recognized the value of

The Schuylkill River Trail in Center City Philadelphia is used not only for running, biking, and strolling, but also for going to and from work, as indicated by the woman in medical attire, probably coming from a hospital on the west side of the river. (Photo by Philip Langdon)

what had been done in the Cotton District and allowed attributes of the district to be introduced into other parts of the city. Unlike conventional zoning codes, form-based codes shape buildings and position them so that they enliven the streets, sidewalks, and other public spaces. The codes recognize the need for a sense of place.

These principles can also be applied in a more piecemeal manner. In some parts of Philadelphia, revised codes now discourage certain buildings, such as townhouses, from having garages on their fronts, dominating the streets and sidewalks. Nothing takes life out of the pedestrian experience like a row of blank garage doors.

For decades, municipalities required new projects to include plenty of off-street parking. That was good for cars and bad for the pedestrian environment. Now, as people increasingly bike, walk, and ride public transit, and in some cases decide not to own a car, municipal standards should be revised to reinforce those trends and create a better cityscape.

Many Americans will resist denser living unless reductions in private outdoor space are offset by increased access to parks, trails, and natural areas. Cities should follow Philadelphia's example, as some are already doing, and create features like the Schuylkill River Trail, which invites people to walk, jog, bike, or commute to work alongside a major urban waterway. Medical employees in hospital scrubs stride to their jobs, sharing the trail with people who are going fishing or heading to basketball courts and softball fields along the route. In most stretches, the trail stays on land. Where land is in short supply, the trail hovers over the water, 50 feet from shore, on a boardwalk 2,000 feet long. The boardwalk is "far enough out," Inga Saffron observed, "that you really feel you're on the water, but not so far that it interferes with boat navigation."[9] For a healthy balance of urbanism, physical fitness, and nature, communities need these kinds of amenities. ·

Designing Streets for People

In 1981, Donald Appleyard wrote *Livable Streets*, a book that showed the impact that different sorts of streets and differing traffic intensities exert on people's lives.[10] Since then, communities have made much progress toward understanding the design and roles of streets. The Complete Streets movement emerged, demanding that streets take into account the needs of the entire spectrum of humanity—pedestrians, cyclists, transit riders, wheelchair users, children, and elderly people—not just motorists. "The Complete Streets movement was started by bicycle advocates but was quickly taken up and advanced by people working in public health, activists for older adults, proponents of smart growth, public transportation agencies, disability advocates, and even real estate agents," wrote Barbara McCann, a cofounder of the National Complete

Fast-moving vehicles remain a lethal challenge, not just for free-range chickens but for people, too. Traffic has to be civilized if we are to walk frequently and to all sorts of destinations. (Drawing by Dhiru A. Thadani)

Streets Coalition.[11] Cyclists, in particular, have benefited from acceptance of Complete Streets principles.

I do most of my errands by bicycle and have ridden in events like the New York Five Boro Bike Tour, so I am attuned to the conditions cyclists encounter. To me, biking is the most refreshing form of transportation there is. As a city lover, however, I have had doubts when bike groups advocated wider streets so that there would be special lanes for cycling. Narrow streets with rows of buildings closely facing each other give the public space a feeling of enclosure. Wider streets can erode the "outdoor room," diminish its charm, and impose a burden on pedestrians, who end up having to cross additional pavement.

The narrow streets of Philadelphia's central neighborhoods function well because their narrowness induces motorists to drive slowly. When the pace of traffic is about 20 miles per hour or less, cyclists and motor vehicles can coexist. A street that seems comfortable to a longtime cyclist like me, however, may not be comfortable for children and women on bikes or for people who are new to cycling.[12] So, there is something to be said for dedicated bike lanes, separate from motor vehicle lanes, especially if a street is already broad or if the traffic is fast or includes many trucks.

A good source of extensively tested bike-route ideas is the Portland Bureau of Transportation, which since the 1980s has been tailoring parts of the city's street network to use by cyclists. The city has more than 70 miles of residential streets designed more for bicycles than for motor vehicles; they are called neighborhood greenways. These greenways also serve pedestrians. Formerly known as bicycle boulevards, the greenways allow cars but are designed to carry no more than two thousand motor vehicles a day. The goal is a daily average of about one thousand motor vehicles.[13]

Usually, a neighborhood greenway has two travel lanes (shared by motorists and cyclists) and two parking lanes. Each travel lane has a shared-lane marking called a "sharrow," typically a silhouette of a bicycle and two broad arrows pointing forward. To discourage motorists from using greenways as shortcuts, speed bumps (gentle enough to be tolerable to cyclists) are commonly installed on these routes. Diverters—barriers such as concrete planters, with gaps for bikes to pass through—further restrict auto access at some points. Where a greenway crosses a busy arterial road, the city paints stripes on the pavement, installs a median island, and erects signs.

At some busy intersections, especially where there are numerous pedestrians or cyclists or where collisions have occurred, the city installs a rapid-flashing beacon; when the button is pressed, the beacon flashes yellow. The device has been found to reduce traffic by up to 40 percent. Portland has further protected cyclists by painting a solid green bar across the pavement of some intersections that bike routes traverse. The green marking alerts motorists to the possibility that cyclists will be coming through.

On a block of NW Marshall Street, a one-way street in Portland's Pearl District, a "contraflow" lane was created, allowing cyclists to travel the direction opposite from motor vehicle traffic. Parking was moved toward the center of the street, placing a row of parked cars between cyclists and moving vehicles. These and other techniques have made Portland the top bike-commuting community in the United States among cities with more than 200,000 inhabitants. In 2014, 7.2 percent of the city's commuters traveled to work by bike, up from 2.8 percent in 2004. The growth in cycling helped reduce the number of vehicle miles driven per person in the region by 12 percent between 2005 and 2015.[14]

University of Arizona planning professor Arthur C. Nelson and four colleagues have documented impressive growth throughout the United States in the number of people walking or biking for errands and walking or biking to work. In 1995, 25 percent of Americans who lived within 1 mile of their job walked or biked to it. By 2009, the figure had jumped to 37 percent. In 1995, 26 percent of those living within 1 mile of an errand destination such as a restaurant or store went there on foot or by bike. By 2009, 42 percent did so.[15] Nelson believes that the number of Americans who want pedestrian-scale communities will keep growing.

"I suspect that fewer than 5 percent of households live within a mile of where they work, though maybe 10 percent live or work within a mile of errands," Nelson told me. "What if we found a way to plan and design communities where a third or even most people could live within a mile of work and live or work within a mile of errands? Just doing this could bring the United States substantially in compliance with the Kyoto Protocol," the 1997 international agreement aimed at reducing climate-damaging greenhouse gas concentrations.

The Problem of High Housing Costs

One of the biggest challenges for walkable communities is that there simply are not enough well-developed, pedestrian-scale, mixed-use neighborhoods to meet the growing demand. Millions of people want to live in such neighborhoods; many of those who act on that desire are converging on comparatively small portions of America's geography. Without intending to do so, they are pushing up prices, sometimes dramatically, in the most beautiful or best located places.

A modest escalation in prices is not necessarily a problem. Residents can afford to pay more for housing when they save on transportation costs, which they can do in neighborhoods where destinations are reachable by foot, bike, or public transit. That's why "location-efficient mortgages," which allow homebuyers to qualify for larger mortgages in communities well connected by transit, have been advocated in recent years by groups such as the Center for Neighborhood Technology.[16]

A rise in housing prices may pose a problem, however, for at least some of the low-income residents of walkable neighborhoods, especially renters. Southwest Center City Philadelphia is a good place to examine the issue in a nuanced way. The influx of new, more affluent residents has brought a number of benefits to Southwest Center City. Incoming residents have attempted to make common cause with their economically struggling neighbors, sometimes by aiding them individually (in ways that range from providing gifts to helping with some of their bills to guiding them through college admissions processes) and sometimes by improving public schools, traffic safety, street sanitation, and public services. Such actions benefit even the poorest residents.

Through organizations such as the Friends of Chester Arthur, new residents, largely middle class and middle to upper income, have upgraded the programs, services, and facilities of schools that are attended mostly by low-income and predominantly African American students. Some of the new residents have enrolled their own children in those schools, which has made the schools slightly less segregated by race and income than they had been. On the other hand, a number of low-income residents have left the neighborhood because they could not afford the rising rents. Some of Southwest Center City's lower-income African American residents have been unhappy about changes of this sort.

In 2015, the Federal Reserve Bank of Philadelphia released a careful study of the effects of revitalization (or gentrification, as its critics call it) in Philadelphia from 2002 to 2014. The study's authors, Lei Ding, Jackelyn Hwang, and Eileen Divringi, found, on average, that people who moved out of gentrifying neighborhoods actually became somewhat better off than they had been before. The changes that arrived with gentrification did not hurt them.[17] (Financial well-being was measured through people's credit scores.)

Daniel Hertz, a commentator at *City Observatory*, summed up two of the main findings of the Philadelphia study as follows. First, in gentrifying neighborhoods, "existing residents are just 0.4 percentage points more likely to move out in a given year than they would be in a non-gentrifying neighborhood." Second, "even in those neighborhoods with the most rapid increases in rents and income, existing residents are just 3.6 percentage points more likely to move."[18]

Many of the people who lived in the gentrifying neighborhoods before the arrival of wealthier residents continued to live there, perhaps in part because new investment and infrastructure improvements made the community more appealing than it had been. The economic status of many of the existing residents improved. In most cases, those who moved out did not go to poorer neighborhoods.

There was also a downside, however. The very poorest who departed tended to end up in low-income neighborhoods, where there were greater problems, such as crime, higher unemployment, and worse-performing schools.

Trends in revitalizing neighborhoods have often been analyzed in terms of the impact on the poor, especially on those who feel compelled to move out. This point certainly deserves attention. There is another aspect to the cost problem, however, that has received too little notice. It is the question of whether enough is being done to make it possible for new people without substantial wealth to move into revitalizing neighborhoods.

After analyzing the Philadelphia study and other gentrification research, Hertz offered this thought:

> When there are problems, they're less likely to be existing residents forced out by rising rents, and more likely to be potential residents who are turned away before they even arrive. The challenge, in neighborhoods that are becoming more affluent as well as ones that already are, is to make sure that there is a sufficient stock of affordable housing (both subsidized and "naturally occurring" at market rate) to accommodate people of whatever means who want to move in. The best way to do that remains to make sure there isn't an overall shortage of housing, and that there's a variety of housing types, from single family homes to apartments of various sizes; and to remain friendly to developers of subsidized housing and people holding housing vouchers.[19]

Hertz's point is critically important because demand for walkable communities is likely to be extremely strong through 2030 and probably beyond. According to Nelson and his colleagues, surveys show that "about half of Americans want to live in walkable communities with mixed uses." Demand for townhouses and other compact forms of housing is going to boom.[20]

Knowledgeable developers, architects, and planners have come up with ideas on what to do about the rising demand and its effect on costs. Jennifer Hurley, a planning consultant based in Center City

Philadelphia, recommends a variety of actions, depending on the location. They include these actions:[21]

- Preserve the affordable housing you already have.
- Lower the cost of production.
- Increase the variety of housing types.
- Shield some units from market pressure.
- Provide subsidies.
- Lower transportation costs.
- Remove or reduce the minimum lot size.
- Remove or reduce parking requirements.
- Make government approvals predictable.
- Upzone to allow higher densities.

Daniel Parolek, an architect at Opticos Design in Berkeley, California, believes that demand for walkable urban living could be partly met
by producing more of what he calls "missing middle" kinds of housing, dwellings that are considerably denser than a single-family house
on a quarter-acre lot but less dense than apartment towers or mid-rise
(several-story) apartment buildings. Among the middle-density housing
types advocated by Parolek are duplexes, triplexes, fourplexes, courtyard apartments, bungalow courts, townhouses, multiplexes, and live/
work units. Such housing can be inserted satisfactorily into many neighborhoods.[22] Urban parking lots could make good sites for some of the
housing Parolek advocates. To his list of compact housing types, Hurley
would add three others: accessory dwelling units (small units created
within a larger dwelling), very small units, and alley houses. Local government can work with neighborhoods groups and developers to make
sure such housing is no longer missing.

In neighborhoods that are expected to shoot up in price because
of strong demand, a nonprofit community land trust is an option to

explore. The land trust acquires and develops a site, retains ownership of the land, and sells the newly built housing units to people who want to live in them; an agreement is signed between the trust and the home buyers so that in future years, when occupants sell their units, part of the profit is turned over to the trust. Thanks to that revenue, the land trust is able keep the units priced lower than would be the case if each seller pocketed the full proceeds.

Another idea is to take action to improve neighborhoods that have some walkable traits but that are languishing. Most cities and towns have neighborhoods that would be more vibrant and appealing if they had more people living in them, along with more stores and restaurants, better transit, and other amenities. Growth in these places, where demand has been too low, could take some of the pressure off the neighborhoods where demand is so high that it is pushing prices to exorbitant levels. The urban resurgence could thus be spread across a larger portion of the town or city rather than staying concentrated in just a few spots.

Some existing residents might oppose intensified development. They might even oppose valuable amenities, such as a new rail transit line, if they think it will drive up housing costs. Those objections might fall by the wayside, however, if local residents and their organizations are given a voice in the development process. That is what has been done in Somerville, Massachusetts, a largely working-class city of 78,000 people north of Boston where the Massachusetts Bay Transportation Authority is extending its Green Line rail service into an area that has lacked it.

The coming of the Green Line is expected to revitalize part of the city, but fears have been voiced that it could also make housing too expensive for some current residents. To address the issue, in 2015 the city, under Mayor Joseph Curtatone, invited Locus, a real estate development program of Smart Growth America, to join local officials and residents in devising a strategy for balanced, beneficial development in the Union Square neighborhood.

Locus, which advocates and researches mixed-income, walkable urban communities, teamed up with a twenty-five-member local committee representing a cross section of Somerville. Together they began working toward "public benefit agreements" to be negotiated with major developers active in Union Square. In return for having their real estate projects approved by the community, the developers will be required to pay toward the transit line and do a range of other things that the community wants. By 2016, the local committee had identified several of the community's priorities, including displacement prevention, affordable housing, jobs and workforce development, open space, and support for small businesses.[23]

"Locus has really engaged the community," said Somerville Planning Director George Proakis. Residents have been asked many questions, such as, "Do you want a library? Do you want a community center?"

Since 1990, the city has required all sizable new housing developments to make at least one-eighth of their units affordable for people of modest means. In Union Square, the requirement may go as high as 20 percent. The overall objectives of the collaboration are to ensure that rail service will arrive, that the community will get development that it is comfortable with, and that social equity goals will be met. In strong real estate markets, a process like this one may help local communities get just the right balance of transit, amenities, residential and commercial development, and affordability.

There is one other perspective on neighborhoods and how they change, improve, confront their problems, and realize their potential. It comes from McKnight and Block, who looked at an Indianapolis neighborhood that is reminiscent of Little Village. Just as Little Village abounds with street vendors, alley mechanics, metal fence makers, day care operators, and other people making a living in whatever way they could, Indianapolis's Broadway United Methodist Church found an entrepreneurial spirit "on every street corner."

As McKnight and Block found, there were people "doing hair on front porches, selling meals from their kitchens, selling candy, doing sewing, fixing cars, caring for pets and children."[24] The church decided to help those people advance in the economy. It set out to help neighbors expand their fledgling businesses and connect with others in nearby neighborhoods to see what they might be able to initiate together.

That example of community organizing highlights something worth keeping in mind: housing costs are only one part of the economic equation. Another, and at least equally important, part is how people can improve their situation by developing a trade, an occupation, or an economic role—something that enables them to keep up with inevitably rising rents. Would it be possible to help the very poor in Southwest Center City Philadelphia get a foothold on the economic ladder? If that can be done, some of those at risk of being displaced might not have to move out at all. They might have the resources to stay in a neighborhood on the upswing.

Individuals, churches, neighborhood associations, wealthy philanthropists, and others could all find reasons to support this endeavor. By working together to develop people's talents and assets, a neighborhood grows more resilient. McKnight and Block subscribe to this view: "A competent community will value what is locally created and sold. It will value the goods and services of a neighbor over a seemingly cheaper version that is imported."[25] Much can be achieved if local people support one another.

That last thought may seem a long way from talking about streets and gathering places, design features that figured prominently in the previous chapters, but in fact these things are all connected. One of the truths observed throughout this book is that a well-functioning walkable community links people to others and reminds them of purposes that make life richer and deeper, if not necessarily easier. If you live in a walkable community, you will know more people, and you will probably know them better than if you live in a house on a big lot, where almost everything you need is an automobile trip away. In a walkable community, you will be more engaged in a network of people and activities outside the door and down the block. In my view, that is how humans are meant to live.

Notes

Introduction

1. To hear Finegar explain why she has focused on creating a neighborhood park, see "Liberty Lands Park in Philadelphia," a brief video from One of Us Films, Oct. 5, 2012, https://vimeo.com/50837214. See also Elisa Lala, "Philadelphia's Plethora of Pocket Parks," *PhillyVoice*, Apr. 6, 2015, http://www.phillyvoice.com/phillys-plethora-pocket-parks/.

2. My estimate of the size of Philadelphia is based on "Plan of the City of Philadelphia and Its Environs Shewing Its Improved Parts" by John Hills (Zebooker Collection, Athenaeum of Philadelphia, 1796), available at http://www.philageohistory.org/rdic-images/view-image.cfm/237-MP-019. At 5 minutes per quarter-mile (today's rule of thumb for walking speed), it would have taken 54 minutes to cover the 2.7 miles from Federal Street in Southwark (Philadelphia's southern edge in 1796) to Poplar Street in Northern Liberties. Because eighteenth-century streets were rougher-surfaced and slower-going than today's, I added several minutes, bringing the trip to a little over an hour. The US Census reports that Philadelphia had a population of 28,522 in 1790 and 41,220 in 1800, second only to New York.

3. Sam Bass Warner Jr., *The Private City: Philadelphia in Three Periods of Its Growth* (Philadelphia: University of Pennsylvania Press, 1968), p. 11.

4. Le Corbusier, *When the Cathedrals Were White* (New York: McGraw-Hill

Paperback Edition, 1964), p. 70. The book told about his 1935 trip to the United States and had its first English-language publication in 1947 in Great Britain. Better known is Le Corbusier's *The Radiant City*, a 1935 book that influenced urban planning worldwide.

5. For a succinct and somewhat critical summary of Le Corbusier's insistence on strict segregation of uses, see Gili Merin, "AD Classics: Ville Radieuse/ Le Corbusier," *Arch Daily Classics*, Aug. 11, 2013, http://www.archdaily .com/411878/ad-classics-ville-radieuse-le-corbusier/.

6. Peter Norton, *Fighting Traffic: The Dawn of the Motor Age in the American City* (Cambridge, MA: MIT Press, 2008), pp. 249–51.

7. My first major article on the compact-development trend was "A Good Place to Live," the cover story of the March 1988 *Atlantic Monthly*.

8. "Take Advantage of Compact Building Design: Highlands' Garden Village, Denver, Colorado," US Environmental Protection Agency, last updated Mar. 29, 2016, https://www.epa.gov/smartgrowth/take-advantage-compact -building-design-highlands-garden-village-denver-colorado.

Chapter 1

1. Amanda Casper reports in "Row Houses" that the first recorded group of rowhouses in the city was Budd's Row, ten houses built around 1691 and later demolished; see *The Encyclopedia of Greater Philadelphia* (Camden, NJ: Rutgers University, 2013), http://philadelphiaencyclopedia.org /archive/row-houses/.

2. Walter Licht, "Rise and Fall of City's Manufacturing Sector," *Philadelphia Inquirer*, Oct. 16, 2011. http://articles.philly.com/2011-10-16/news /30286372_1_manufacturing-sector-products-goods.

3. H. G. (Buzz) Bissinger, *A Prayer for the City: The True Story of a Mayor and Five Heroes in a Race Against Time* (New York: Random House, 1997).

4. Paul R. Levy and Lauren M. Gilchrist, "Downtown Rebirth: Documenting the Live-Work Dynamic in 21st Century U.S. Cities," 2013, pp. 22, 23, 27. This report, prepared for the International Downtown Association by the Philadelphia Center City District, said that 57,239 people were living in Philadelphia's "commercial downtown." Adding a half-mile adjacent area brings the total to 107,853. If the adjacent area is extended to one mile, the total residential population rises to 170,467.

5. Central Philadelphia Development Corporation and Center City District, "Center City Reports: Pathways to Job Growth," Jan. 2014, p. 13.

6. Paul Levy, Center City District, e-mail correspondence, Nov. 3, 2016.

7. "The Success of Downtown Living: Expanding the Boundaries of Center City," *Center City Developments*, a publication of the Center City District and Central Philadelphia Development Corp., Apr. 2002, pp. 4–5.

8. See Susan Warner, "The Developer King of Center City," *Philadelphia Inquirer*, Feb. 26, 1990, http://articles.philly.com/1990-02-26/business /25880613_1_office-building-developer-center-city; and Patrick Kerkstra, "How Paul Levy Created Center City," *Philadelphia Magazine*, Nov. 22, 2013, http://www.phillymag.com/articles/paul-levy-created-center-city /?all=1.

9. Paul Levy, "Diversifying Downtown from the Ground Up," *IEDC Economic Development Journal*, Spring 2013, p. 8.

10. Karen Heller, "Getting Homeless Back on Track with Apartments," *Philadelphia Inquirer*, Apr. 17, 2014, http://articles.philly.com/2014-04-17 /news/49188473_1_pathways-rate-sam-tsemberis.

11. Levy, "Diversifying Downtown," p. 9.

12. Inga Saffron, "Changing Skyline: Thriving Philadelphia Neighborhood Rises from High-Rise Rubble," *Philadelphia Inquirer*, Aug. 18, 2012, http://articles.philly.com/2012-08-18/news/33249381_1_hawthorne-em powerment-coalition-hope-vi-torti-gallas-partners.

13. Tower Investments corporate profile, accessed Oct. 3, 2016, http://www .towerdev.com/about-tower.html.

14. Kim Bernardin, "Learning from the Piazza at Broad & Washington," *Hidden City Philadelphia*, Mar. 23, 2016, http://hiddencityphila.org/2016/03 /learning-from-the-piazza-at-broad-washington/.

15. Bernardin, "Learning from the Piazza."

16. Sandy Smith, "The Piazza Gets New Name, Adds Co-Working to the Mix," *Philadelphia Magazine*, June 1, 2016, http://www.phillymag.com /property/2016/06/01/schmidts-commons-adds-co-working-space/.

17. Danya Henninger, "The Spot: Standard Tap," *Philly.com*, Jan. 26, 2015, http://www.philly.com/philly/blogs/food_department/The-Spot-Standard -Tap-Northern-Liberties.html.

18. Craig LaBan, "Talking 'the Avenue' with Lynn Rinaldi," *Philadelphia*

Inquirer, Apr. 20, 2015, http://articles.philly.com/2015-04-20/news/6130 8084_1_paradiso-restaurant-arcade.

19. Tom Ferrick Jr., "City Blocks: How East Passyunk Ave. Got Hot," Metropolis, June 27, 2010, http://www.phlmetropolis.com/2010/06/post.php.

20. "Singing Fountain" review, Yelp, Aug. 9, 2014, http://www.yelp.com/biz/singing-fountain-philadelphia.

21. PARC's predecessor organization, Citizens Alliance for Better Neighborhoods, was an instrument of the corrupt State Senator Vincent Fumo, who was sentenced to a federal prison term. Philadelphia journalist Tom Ferrick Jr. nonetheless argued that the alliance's revitalization strategy was well conceived and benefited the neighborhood. See Tom Ferrick Jr., "City Blocks: How East Passyunk Ave. Got Hot," *Metropolis Philadelphia*, June 27, 2010, http://www.phlmetropolis.com/2010/06/post.php.

22. Andrew Dalzell, in *Evergreens: A Neighborhood History* (Philadelphia: South of South Neighborhood Association, 2013), p. 37, traces planning for the expressway back to 1934. There was discussion about running the highway through Lombard Street, but by 1959, South Street was the officially preferred route.

23. This and later information from Dalzell is mainly from *Evergreens*, pp. 39–40.

24. *State of Center City Philadelphia 2014* (Philadelphia: Center City District and Central Philadelphia Development Corp., 2014), p. 51.

25. Inga Saffron, "Changing Skyline: Bolstering School for the Neighborhood," *Philadelphia Inquirer*, July 6, 2013, http://articles.philly.com/2013-07-06/entertainment/40393929_1_friends-group-philadelphia-school-district-ivy-olesh.

Chapter 2

1. Ray Oldenburg, *The Great Good Place* (St. Paul, MN: Paragon House, 1989), p. xi.

2. DataHaven, a New Haven nonprofit organization, lists East Rock's population as 9,072 and places the neighborhood's western boundary at Whitney Avenue. I and others think that the western boundary is more logically Prospect Street. Mark Abraham at DataHaven estimates this revised area,

minus the Cedar Hill area east of East Rock Park, as having about 9,100 residents.

3. Michael Morand, "University Renews Yale Homebuyer Program for Another Two Years," *Yale News*, Dec. 7, 2015, http://news.yale.edu/2015/12/07 /university-renews-yale-homebuyer-program-another-two-years.

4. Mobility figures are from Mary Buchanan, "Table: 2014 New Haven Neighborhood Estimates," DataHaven, Feb. 10, 2016, http://ctdatahaven .org/data-resources/table-2014-new-haven-neighborhood-estimates.

5. Personal communication with Mark Abraham, DataHaven, Nov. 9, 2016.

6. Oldenburg, *The Great Good Place*, p. 284.

Chapter 3

1. The history of Sam's Army & Navy is discussed in "From Russia with Love: The Borofsky Legacy, from the Old Country to Brattleboro," in *The Commons Online*, Apr. 6, 2011, http://www.commonsnews.org/site/site05 /story.php?articleno=2828&page=3#.Vxj-42NOrXU.

2. "Artist's Statement," accessed Oct. 3, 2016, http://larrysimons.com/artist .html.

3. Norman Runnion, retired managing editor of the *Brattleboro Reformer*, said that an attitude of "hospitality to strangers and interest in their diversity" was first instilled in the area's residents by nineteenth-century "water-cure" establishments. That outlook, he said, was reinforced by the Brattleboro Retreat, which helped ensure that "Brattleboro became accustomed to people of difference. . . ." See Norman Runnion, "London, Paris, New York . . . Brattleboro," *Vermont Magazine*, Sept.–Oct. 1990, p. 44.

4. Runnion, "London," p. 45.

5. Stacy Mitchell, "Brattleboro Group Urges Residents to Support Local Merchants," *Independent Business* (Institute for Local Self-Reliance), Feb. 1, 2004, http://ilsr.org/brattleboro-group-urges-residents-support-local-mer chants/.

6. John Curran, Associated Press, "Local Hardware Stores Outlast Home Depot in One Vermont Town," *Pittsburgh Post-Gazette*, May 3, 2008, http://www.post-gazette.com/business/businessnews/2008/05/03/Local -hardware-stores-outlast-Home-Depot-in-one-Vermont-town/stories /200805030177.

7. Dave Eisenstadter, *Embattled Brattleboro: How a Vermont Town Endured a Year of Fire, Murder and Hurricane Irene* (East Middlebury, VT: Surry Cottage Books, 2012), p. 75. Much of my discussion of Brooks House is drawn from Eisenstadter's book and from communication with Robert Stevens.

8. Susan Keese, "Brattleboro's Brooks House Prepares for Colleges' Arrival," Vermont Public Radio, July 3, 2014, http://digital.vpr.net/post/brattlebor os-brooks-house-prepares-colleges-arrival#stream/0.

9. "Brattleboro, Vermont: Vermont Downtown Action Team Report," Vermont Department of Housing and Community Development, Aug. 1, 2014, pp. 43–45, http://accd.vermont.gov/sites/accdnew/files/documents /CPR-VDAT-Report-Brattleboro.pdf.

10. Maddi Shaw, "Brattleboro Group Hosts Forum on Pedestrian and Cyclist Safety," *Brattleboro Reformer*, May 4, 2016, http://www.reformer.com/lat estnews/ci_29852012/brattleboro-group-hosts-forum-pedestrian-and-cy clist-safety.

11. "Vermont Downtown Action Team Report" found (p. 16) that in Brattleboro's primary trade area, median household income was $40,973, whereas Vermont's median was $53,422 and the US median was $52,762. The secondary trade area, made up of eight zip codes, had a median household income of $51,115, more on par with state and national figures.

12. Howard Weiss-Tisman, "Brattleboro: Struggling to Keep Downtown Viable," *Brattleboro Reformer*, June 26, 2015, http://www.reformer.com/local news/ci_28390541/brattleboro-struggling-keep-downtown-viable.

13. "Vermont Downtown Action Team Report," p. 21.

Chapter 4

1. Much of this information on the first one hundred years of Little Village's history came from Frank S. Magallon, *Chicago's Little Village: Lawndale-Crawford* (Mount Pleasant, SC: Arcadia, 2010).

2. Eric Klinenberg, *Heat Wave: A Social Autopsy of Disaster in Chicago* (Chicago: University of Chicago Press, 2002), p. 16.

3. Klinenberg, *Heat Wave*, p. 87.

4. Klinenberg, *Heat Wave*, p. 91.

5. An alternative explanation for Little Village's few deaths—offered by local political leader Jesus Garcia—is that the Mexicans had a custom of check-

ing on one another to make sure that they were well. The Bohemians had much the same practice, said Chicago historian Dominic Pacyga. See Dominic A. Pacyga, *Chicago: A Biography* (Chicago: University of Chicago Press, 2009), p. 390, for a brief discussion of Mexican immigration to Chicago. Whether the custom of "checking" outweighs Klinenberg's hypothesis about busy commercial streets and public places saving people's lives is not clear to me.

6. Antonio Olivo, "Immigrant Family in U.S. Sees Better Life Back Home," *Chicago Tribune*, Jan. 6, 2013, http://www.chicagotribune.com/news/mex ico-reverse-migration-20130106-story.html.

7. Edgar Leon, "Business of the Month: Azucar," Enlace Chicago e-newsletter, May 2012.

8. Kari Lydersen, "Chicago without Coal," *Chicago Reader*, Oct. 14, 2010, http://www.chicagoreader.com/chicago/chicago-coal-pollution-fisk-state -line-plants/Content?oid=2558655.

9. Julie Wernau, "Closure of Chicago's Crawford, Fisk Electric Plants Ends Coal Era," *Chicago Tribune*, Aug. 30, 2012, http://articles.chicagotribune .com/2012-08-30/business/chi-closure-of-chicagos-crawford-fisk-electric -plants-ends-coal-era-20120830_1_fisk-and-crawford-midwest-genera tion-coal-plants.

10. Leonor Vivanco, "Long-Awaited Little Village Park to Open," *Chicago Tribune*, Dec. 11, 2014, http://www.chicagotribune.com/news/ct-little -village-park-talk-1211-20141211-story.html.

11. "La Villita Park Opens at Former Celotex Site," US Environmental Protection Agency, Jan. 2015, https://www3.epa.gov/region5/cleanup/celotex /pdfs/celotex-fs-201501.pdf.

12. "Transit Victory," LVEJO website, accessed Oct. 4, 2016, http://lvejo.org /our-accomplishments/transit-victory/.

13. Robert J. Sampson, *Great American City: Chicago and the Enduring Neighborhood Effect* (Chicago: University of Chicago Press, 2012), pp. 253, 259.

14. The Two Sixes began in 1964, originally as a baseball team, and evolved into a gang, some of whose members sold drugs, according to the website ChicagoGangs.org, accessed Oct. 4, 2016, http://chicagogangs.org/index .php?pr=TWO_SIX.

15. See James C. Howell and John P. Moore, "History of Street Gangs in the United States," National Gang Center Bulletin, May 2010, pp. 5–9, https://www.nationalgangcenter.gov/content/documents/history-of-street -gangs.pdf. A landmark first published in 1927, still in print at the University of Chicago Press, is *The Gang: A Study of 1,313 Gangs in Chicago* by sociologist Frederick Milton Thrasher.

16. One who blames whites for the initial formation of gangs is Jesus Salazar, outreach supervisor for Ceasefire, a Little Village antiviolence organization. In an interview with the *Gate News* published on July 3, 2014, by the Back of the Yards Neighborhood Council, Salazar said, "Before the minorities started moving in, the majority were white people and when you would go into their neighborhood or move into their neighborhood, they basically acted violent towards you"; see http://www.thegatenewspa per.com/2014/07/drogas-y-pandillas-en-la-villita-una-vista-desde-la-base/. Redistributed as "Drugs & Gangs in Little Village: View from the Ground," *SJNN* (Social Justice News Nexus), July 15, 2014, http://sjnnchicago.org /drugs-and-gangs-in-little-village-a-view-from-the-ground/.

17. "Border Mentality: 26th Street," *El Arco Press*, Oct. 31, 2013, http://www .chicagonow.com/el-arco-press/2013/10/border-mentality/.

18. "Border Mentality."

19. Maureen Kelleher, "Schools CEO Funds Safety at Little Village Lawndale," Local Initiatives Support Corporation, Chicago's New Communities Program, Mar. 13, 2009, http://www.newcommunities.org/news/articleDetail .asp?objectID=1389.

20. Mitchell Armentrout, "Paseo Trail to Connect Pilsen, Little Village Neighborhoods," *Chicago Sun-Times*, Mar. 20, 2016, http://chicago.suntimes .com/news/paseo-trail-to-connect-pilsen-little-village-neighborhoods/.

Chapter 5

1. Philip Langdon, "How Portland Does It," *The Atlantic*, Nov. 1992, pp. 134–41.

2. Jane Comerford, *A History of Northwest Portland: From the River to the Hills* (Portland, OR: Dragonfly-Press-PDX, 2011), pp. 78, 82. Comerford reports that years after coining the Pearl District's name, Thomas Augus-

tine changed his story and claimed that the district was named for a world traveler from Ethiopia. Al Solheim, in a Sept. 21, 2014, e-mail to me, said that the Ethiopian story is "not correct."

3. Jeremiah Chamberlin, "Inside Indie Bookstores: Powell's Books in Portland, Oregon," *Poets & Writers*, Mar.–Apr. 2010, http://www.pw.org/content/inside_indie_bookstores_powell_s_books_in_portland_oregon?article_page=2.

4. Nigel Jaquiss, "Homer's Odyssey," *Willamette Week*, July 29, 2003, http://www.wweek.com/portland/article-2307-homers-odyssey.html.

5. The affordability requirement appears in Exhibit D-2 of the amended contract of Mar. 12, 1999, http://www.pdc.us/Libraries/Document_Library/Hoyt_St_Property_Agreement_pdf.sflb.ashx.

6. Ed Langlois, "Portland Organizing Project Seeks to Broaden Its Base of Influence, Concern," *Catholic Sentinel*, Feb. 12, 1999, http://www.catholicsentinel.org/main.asp?SectionID=2&SubSectionID=35&ArticleID=3562.

7. Developer Homer Williams said that he and others worried that placing rocks and steps in Jamison Square would turn the park into a magnet for skateboarding teenagers. To avoid that, landscape architect Peter Walker added flowing water, which had the unintended consequence of making the park a busy play area for children. See Peter Korn, "Oops!," *Portland Tribune*, Oct. 29, 2008, http://portlandtribune.com/component/content/article?id=77203.

8. Charles Kelley, "Building Equity with the Creative Class in Portland and Orlando," presentation to the American Planning Association, Phoenix, AZ, Mar. 29, 2016, https://www.dropbox.com/s/fy4e8rq0iog1o1x/APA_Innovation%20Presentation_3.29.16.pptx?dl=0. For another assessment of increased density, see Randy Gragg, "Reflecting on the Past, Present, and Future of Portland's Pearl District," *Portland Monthly*, Oct. 5, 2015, http://www.pdxmonthly.com/articles/2015/10/5/past-present-and-future-of-portlands-pearl-district.

9. ECONorthwest, "Technical Memo—Portland Streetcar Development Impact Study," Aug. 4, 2015, pp. 1, 5, 6. See also https://storage.googleapis.com/streetcar/files/Infographic-1-Final.pdf.

10. "Tumblin' Down: Lovejoy Viaduct a Casualty of Progress," *Daily Journal*

of Commerce, Aug. 19, 1999, http://djcoregon.com/news/1999/08/19/tum
blin-down-lovejoy-viaduct-a-casualty-of-progress/.

11. A spare-no-expense modernist design in one of the depot buildings is
    described in Randy Gragg, "Drawn to Perfection: A Townhouse Rehab Fuses
    Bold Design and Precise Workmanship," *The Oregonian*, May 1, 2003,
    pp. 1, 20–29, http://www.fhzal.com/works/010402/gragg-030501.asp.

12. Gragg, "Reflecting."

13. Brad Schmidt, "Hoyt Street Properties Fails to Deliver Enough Afford-
    able Housing under Portland's Pearl District Development Deal," *The
    Oregonian*, Aug. 20, 2014, http://www.oregonlive.com/portland/index
    .ssf/2014/08/hoyt_street_properties_fails_t.html.

14. Jon Bell, "'Deeply Affordable' Housing Project Set to Rise in the Pearl,"
    Portland Business Journal, Oct. 14, 2015, http://www.bizjournals.com
    /portland/blog/real-estate-daily/2015/10/deeply-affordable-housing-proj
    ect-set-to-rise-in.html. The project has since been modified.

15. Janie Har, "Is 20 Percent of Housing in Portland's Pearl District Really
    Affordable?" *PolitiFact Oregon*, Nov. 18, 2011, http://www.politifact.com
    /oregon/statements/2011/nov/18/tom-hughes/20-percent-housing-port
    lands-pearl-district-really/.

16. Denis C. Theriault, "Landmark Housing Bill Wins Final Approval from
    Oregon Legislature," *The Oregonian*, Mar. 3, 2016, http://www.oregonlive
    .com/politics/index.ssf/2016/03/affordable_housing_mandates_wi.html.
    See also Luke Hammill, "Portland Signals Support for New Construction
    Excise Tax," *The Oregonian*, June 16, 2016, http://www.oregonlive.com
    /portland/index.ssf/2016/06/portland_signals_support_for_n.html.

17. Andrew Theen, "Portland's $258.4 Million Housing Bond Wins (Election
    Results)," *The Oregonian*, Nov. 8, 2016, http://www.oregonlive.com/pol
    itics/index.ssf/2016/11/portlands_2584_million_housing.html. See also
    Bruce Stephenson, "$258 Million Affordable Housing Bond Will Be a Test
    for Portland (Opinion)," *Oregon Live*, July 5, 2016, http://www.oregon
    live.com/opinion/index.ssf/2016/07/258_million_affordable_housing
    .html.

18. "Pearl Lofts, Portland, Oregon," *Urban Land Institute Project Reference File*
    26, no. 6 (Apr.–June 1996).

19. In 2015 and 2016, Stephenson produced a lively blog that examined

many aspects of the Pearl District; see "Living New Urbanism: Stepping into Sustainability," http://livingnewurbanism.blogspot.com/search?up dated-min=2015-01-01T00:00:00-08:00&updated-max=2016-01-01T 00:00:00-08:00&max-results=19.

20. Iain MacKenzie, "Going Tall: New Projects Complete the North Pearl District," *Portland Architecture* blog, http://chatterbox.typepad.com/portland architecture/2015/10/going-tall-new-projects-complete-the-north-pearl -district.html.

21. Michael Mehaffy, "Has Portland Lost Its Way?" *Planetizen*, May 25, 2016, http://www.planetizen.com/node/86508/has-portland-lost-its-way.

22. Michael Mehaffy, "5 Key Themes Emerging from the 'New Science of Cities,'" *CityLab*, Sept. 19, 2014, http://www.citylab.com/design/2014/09/5 -key-themes-emerging-from-the-new-science-of-cities/380233/.

Chapter 6

1. Marilyn Avery, "The Placemaker," *Progressive Architecture*, June 1995, p. 106, http://www.cottondistrictms.com/progressive-architecture/.

2. Quote about "unwise location" is from Dan Camp, "History of the Cotton District," posted on the Cotton District website, http://www.cottondistrict ms.com/history-of-cd/, and accessed Oct. 4, 2016.

3. Avery, "The Placemaker," p. 108.

4. Victor Dover, "Dan Camp's Cotton District," *Council Report III*, Congress for New Urbanism, 2003, p. 8, https://www.cnu.org/sites/default/files /Council%20Report%20III%20and%20IV_HR.pdf. In *Council Report III*, see also Dan Camp, "A Renewal of a Mississippi Neighborhood," p. 6; Kevin Klinkenberg, "Dan Camp and the Cotton District," p. 9; and Brian Herrmann, "Psychosociology of the Cotton District," pp. 9, 38.

5. Dover, "Dan Camp's Cotton District."

6. Carl Smith, "Form-Based Codes Guiding Numerous Urban Developments," *Commercial Dispatch*, Nov. 3, 2015, http://www.cdispatch.com /news/article.asp?aid=45975.

7. As long ago as 1994, Brad German, in "Dateline Mississippi—Dan Camp's Slum Renewal Project in Starkville, Mississippi" (*Builder*, May 1994), asserted that it was "hard to see how Camp could survive in a heavily regulated market"; see http://www.cottondistrictms.com/dateline-mississippi/.

8. The Project for Lean Urbanism is managed by the Center for Applied Transect Studies and has received financial support from the John S. and James L. Knight Foundation and the Kresge Foundation. See http://leanurbanism .org/about/.
9. See Anthony Flint, "Why Andres Duany Is So Focused on Making 'Lean Urbanism' a Thing," *CityLab*, Mar. 14, 2014, http://www.citylab.com /design/2014/03/why-andres-duany-so-focused-making-lean-urbanism -thing/8635/.
10. Flint, "Why Andres Duany Is So Focused."

Conclusion

1. Carl Abbott, "The Oregon Planning Style," in *Planning the Oregon Way: A Twenty-Year Evaluation*, edited by Carl Abbott, Deborah A. Howe, and Sy Adler (Corvallis: Oregon State University Press, 1994), pp. 206–8, http://pdxscholar.library.pdx.edu/cgi/viewcontent.cgi?article=1049&con text=usp_fac.
2. Norman Runnion, "London, Paris, New York . . . Brattleboro," *Vermont Magazine*, Sept.–Oct. 1990, p. 44.
3. John McKnight and Peter Block, *The Abundant Community: Awakening the Power of Families and Neighborhoods* (Oakland, CA: Berrett-Koehler, 2012), pp. 18, 71–72.
4. Research by Steven Reed Johnson, the League of Women Voters, and others on Portland's neighborhood system and the Office of Neighborhood Involvement is found on the website https://www.portlandoregon.gov /oni/38596.
5. Steven Reed Johnson, "The Myth and Reality of Portland," in *The Portland Edge*, edited by Connie P. Ozawa (Washington, DC: Island Press, 2004), p. 116.
6. Brooke Jarvis, "Building the World We Want: Interview with Mark Lakeman," *YES! Magazine*, May 12, 2010, http://www.yesmagazine.org/happi ness/building-the-world-we-want-interview-with-mark-lakeman.
7. Alyse Nelson and Tim Shuck, "City Repair Project Case Study," University of Washington, 2005, http://courses.washington.edu/activism/cityrepair .htm.

8. Mike Lydon and Anthony Garcia, *Tactical Urbanism: Short-Term Action for Long-Term Change* by (Washington, DC: Island Press, 2015), p. xxi.

9. Inga Saffron, "Phila.'s New Gem: A Stroll on the Schuylkill," *Philadelphia Inquirer*, Sept. 29, 2014, http://articles.philly.com/2014-09-29/news/54404594_1_high-line-south-street-bridge-south-philadelphia.

10. Donald Appleyard, *Livable Streets* (Berkeley: University of California Press, 1981).

11. Barbara McCann, *Completing Our Streets: The Transition to Safe and Inclusive Transportation Networks* (Washington, DC: Island Press, 2013), p. 25.

12. Studies have found that because of safety concerns, women are more averse than men to bicycling in or near motor vehicle traffic. Women tend to prefer a "cycle track" (a bike route that is physically separated from motor traffic and distinct from the sidewalk) or an off-street bike path. China's extensive system of cycle tracks has proven especially popular with women. See J. Garrard, G. Rose, and S. K. Lo, "Promoting Transportation Cycling for Women: The Role of Bicycle Infrastructure," *Preventive Medicine* 1, no. 46 (2008): 55–59, http://www.ncbi.nlm.nih.gov/pubmed/17698185; and A. Lusk, X. Wen, and L. Zhou, "Gender and Used/Preferred Differences of Bicycle Routes, Parking, Intersection Signals, and Bicycle Type: Professional Middle Class Preferences in Hangzhou, China," *Journal of Transport and Health* 1 (2014): 124–33, http://www.sciencedirect.com/science/article/pii/S2214140514000334.

13. Executive Summary, "Portland's Neighborhood Greenways Assessment Report," 2015, https://www.portlandoregon.gov/transportation/article/542725.

14. "You Are Here: A Snapshot of How the Portland Region Gets Around," *Metro News*, Apr. 18, 2016, http://www.oregonmetro.gov/news/you-are-here-snapshot-how-portland-region-gets-around.

15. See Arthur C. Nelson, Gail Meakins, Deanne Weber, Shyam Kannan, and Reid Ewing, "The Tragedy of Unmet Demand for Walking and Biking," *Urban Lawyer* 45, no. 3 (Summer 2013): 615–30.

16. Development of location-efficient mortgages started in 1995 in a research program led by the Center for Neighborhood Technology (CNT), the Natural Resources Defense Council, and the Surface Transportation Policy Project. Between 2000 and about 2006, approximately two thousand such

mortgages were written. They did not end up in foreclosure. Such mortgages ceased being offered after the 2008 global financial crisis. In November 2016, Scott Bernstein at CNT said that some form of location-efficient mortgage may soon be reintroduced. See http://www.cnt.org/projects/re thinking-mortgages.

17. Lei Ding, Jackelyn Hwang, and Eileen Divringi, "Gentrification and Residential Mobility in Philadelphia," Federal Reserve Bank of Philadelphia, Dec. 2015, p. 25, https://www.philadelphiafed.org/community-develop ment/publications/discussion-papers. See also Tanvi Misra, "Gentrification Is Not Philly's Biggest Problem," *CityLab*, May 20, 2016, http://www .citylab.com/housing/2016/05/gentrification-is-not-phillys-biggest-prob lem/483656/.

18. Daniel Hertz, "What's Really Going On in Gentrifying Neighborhoods?" *City Observatory*, Oct. 28, 2015, http://cityobservatory.org/whats-really -going-on-in-gentrifying-neighborhoods/.

19. Hertz, "What's Really Going On."

20. Arthur C. Nelson, *Reshaping Metropolitan America: Development Trends and Opportunities to 2030* (Washington, DC: Island Press, 2013), pp. 3, 36.

21. Jennifer Hurley, "A Smart Growth Approach to Affordable Housing," Coruway Film Institute, presentation in Portsmouth, NH, Jan. 28, 2016, https://www.youtube.com/watch?v=hagol16v8Ao.

22. Opticos Design, "Missing Middle: Responding to the Demand for Walkable Urban Living," http://missingmiddlehousing.com.

23. "City of Somerville, MA and LOCUS Release Results and Next Steps of Program to Balance Economic Growth and Social Equity in Union Square," Smart Growth America, May 3, 2016, http://www.smartgrowthamerica .org/2016/05/03/city-of-somerville-ma-and-locus-release-results-and -next-steps-of-program-to-balance-economic-growth-and-social-equity -in-union-square/.

24. McKnight and Block, *The Abundant Community*, p. 108.

25. McKnight and Block, *The Abundant Community*, p. 98.

Index